RESCUING
The LANGUAGE of FAITH

HOLY VOCABULARY

MICHAEL KELLEY

Published by LifeWay Press®
© 2010 Michael Kelley

ISBN: 978-1-4158-6900-0
Item: 005271631

Dewey Decimal Classification Number: 230
Subject Heading: CHRISTIANITY—DOCTRINES \ VOCABULARY—RELIGIOUS ASPECTS

Printed in the United States of America.

Leadership and Adult Publishing
LifeWay Church Resources
One LifeWay Plaza
Nashville, Tennessee 37234-0175

We believe the Bible has God for its author; salvation for its end; and truth, without any mixture of error, for its matter and that all Scripture is totally true and trustworthy. The 2000 statement of *The Baptist Faith and Message* is our doctrinal guideline.

Cover design by Brezinka Design Co.

TABLE OF CONTENTS

ICON LEGEND

 Things to
listen to

Things
to watch

 Expanding on
biblical concepts

Fun facts and useful
tidbits of information

Digging deeper into
study concepts

 Available tools for
group leaders

On the
Web

MEET THE AUTHOR
MICHAEL KELLEY

My name is Michael Kelley. I live in Nashville,
Tennessee, with my wife, Jana, and our three kids:
Joshua, Andi, and Christian. We live in a house that
was built in 1955, so I'm progressively learning how
to change light bulbs. I grew up in Texas and then
moved to Birmingham, Alabama, where I earned a
Master of Divinity at Beeson Divinity School. Now
I'm an author, editor, and communicator along with
continually learning how to be a husband and father.

Why *Holy Vocabulary*? Because I have the tendency
to use a lot of words when I dialogue about my
faith without considering what they mean. I assume
that everyone speaks the language of the Christian
subculture, so I don't have to think about what "sin"
is or what it means to "repent." Except I do have to
think about it, and you do, too.

My hope and prayer is that this study is the means
by which we become reacquainted—or acquainted
for the first time—with the language of faith.
Knowing what these words mean will do more
than make us sound intelligent. These words can
be the means by which we're drawn into a deeper
walk with Jesus and a more intimate appreciation
of everything God is. The words in this book frame
our Christian experience; they enable us to put into
words what we experience. At least they do for me,
and I hope they will for you as well.

Feel free to drop by and visit me online, where I
blog daily at *michaelkelleyministries.wordpress.com*.

HOLY VOCABULARY

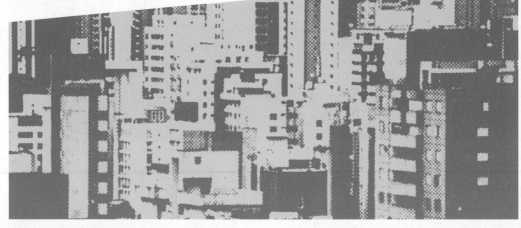

RESCUING THE LANGUAGE OF FAITH

Klingon is an actual language. That's right—the war-loving, spear-toting villains of *Star Trek* world have their own official language. And people speak it. In fact, you can even get a college scholarship if you're familiar with the alien language.[1] Similarly, there are people who write letters to one another in Elvish, a language that originated in *The Lord of the Rings*.

More common is the vocabulary shared between people who know a thing or two about cars. Enter into their conversation and you might hear stuff about carburetors and engine blocks. There's also a culture of couponers, who talk about BOGO discounts and rebates, and inform one another about which store is selling Pampers® wipes at a discounted rate this week.

Stick me in any of these situations and I'd be totally lost, completely uncomfortable, and speechless. But if you consider yourself part of the subculture of *Star Trek, The Lord of the Rings,* auto mechanics, or thrifty shoppers, you might feel right at home.

Subcultures are like that. They have their own language, dress, and customs. If you're a part of that subculture, you've integrated the speech, clothes, and food into your daily life, and now you don't even give it a second thought. You freely communicate in Klingon with your friends, not worrying too much about the unenlightened individuals who haven't bothered to pick up their own pronunciation guide.

But if you're the unenlightened individual observing a subculture from the outside, what you see means relatively little to you. You see groups of people convinced that how they communicate with one another is normal. However you, the outsider, hear nothing but confusing rhetoric. You live in the real world, where people actually speak languages that others can understand.

THE CHRISTIAN SUBCULTURE

Subcultures are everywhere. Chances are you belong to at least one, even if you don't realize it. You might be a member of the technology subculture. Or the home school subculture. Or the SEC football subculture.

Me? I'm a card-carrying member of the Christian subculture. We have our own rock stars, communicators, authors, schools, radio stations, and lines of apparel. We even have our own arguments that mean relatively little to anyone outside the subculture. The Christian subculture is filled with customs, dress, food, and a vocabulary of holy words that, to the common observer, are as unfamiliar as the cliffs of Mordor or the parts under the hood of a car.

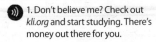 1. Don't believe me? Check out *kli.org* and start studying. There's money out there for you.

A non-Christian walking into the church today might as well be stepping into a comic book convention. They would likely find a group of people so entrenched in their own subculture that they don't even think about what they're saying, singing, or preaching. After all, they all understand each other; they're speaking the same language.

THE CHRISTIAN SUBCULTURE IS FILLED WITH CUSTOMS, DRESS, FOOD, AND A VOCABULARY OF HOLY WORDS THAT, TO THE COMMON OBSERVER, ARE AS UNFAMILIAR AS THE CLIFFS OF MORDOR.

Subcultures do have a positive side—they're safe. They're comfortable. They're easy. They're part of who you are. Inside the comfort of a subculture, you don't really have to think a lot about what you're saying or the meaning behind it. For example, if you're in the Christian subculture, it's natural to assume that everyone around you knows what it means to be "saved," they know how to "repent," and they know what it means to call God "holy." So you just rattle on, firmly entrenched in the familiar.

The problem is, not everyone does understand. Within the church, we operate under the assumption that people know what we mean when we talk about "church" things. For 2,000 years, we've been using classic words of the faith to describe what Christianity is all about. But in those 2,000 years, there have been countless arguments, discrepancies, and qualifications about these terms. The same terms that "everyone" understands. I can't help but wonder if we, members of the church, even know what we're saying anymore.

And that's the danger of living inside of a subculture—you can get so accustomed to certain aspects of that subculture that they lose their meaning. The Lord's Supper becomes just a snack between the songs and the sermon, and the Bible becomes the hard surface to put your intra-worship doodle pad on.

UNCOVERING THE VALUE OF OUR WORDS

As the Christian subculture has grown, somewhere along the line we've stopped thinking about what we say we believe. I think it's time to bust up the subculture. To start thinking. To remember. To stop living on the surface. And one of the ways we do that is by rescuing the language we use to talk about our faith. These words—such as holy, sin, lost, fruit, justice, mission—are important words. They are essential descriptions of the Christian faith. But they've been hijacked by familiarity and have lost the punch of their meaning. Let's get them back.

Holy Vocabulary is for all of us—those inside the Christian subculture and those outside of it—because all of us need to know what these words mean. All of us need to remember who God is and what He has done for us in Christ. And that means starting to understand this language so freely spoken inside the walls of the church.

The seven sessions of this book are divided into the classic categories of systematic theology—God, humanity, Jesus, the Holy Spirit, church, the end times, and Scripture. Within each session we'll unpack five of the key terms associated with that topic. *Holy Vocabulary* certainly doesn't cover all the terms of faith; it barely scratches the surface of our language. But it does provide a good foundation—a starting point, encouraging us all to know what we mean when we start talking about God, or the Holy Spirit, or even the end times described in Revelation.

If we can reach the point where we truly understand what we mean when we talk about the essential elements of Christianity, then maybe anyone encountering it for the first time won't feel like they just stepped into the origin story of Wolverine or the complicated universe of Green Lantern. And maybe those of us so ingrained in the subculture already can actually start to understand the meaning behind the words we throw around each and every day.

ALL OF US NEED TO REMEMBER WHO GOD IS AND WHAT HE HAS DONE FOR US IN CHRIST. AND THAT MEANS STARTING TO UNDERSTAND THIS LANGUAGE SO FREELY SPOKEN INSIDE THE WALLS OF THE CHURCH.

It's a language jailbreak; we're busting loose from the confines of the familiar and taking the words of the faith with us. In the end, we'll find the rock-solid truth of faith buried beneath the overused terminology we so easily take for granted.

HOW TO USE THIS BOOK

Each session of *Holy Vocabulary* focuses on a main category of Christian doctrine and five words commonly used when talking about that topic.

• Go at your own pace.
• Try studying a word a day. (If that's too much, give yourself a couple of days.)
• Study Scripture passages associated with each word.
• Think through the questions. Jot down any thoughts, ideas, or questions you want to remember.
• For the best experience, get together with a group and discuss what you're learning and discovering.

IN THE BEGINNING GOD . . .

Where do you start if you want to learn about God? Do you look first to nature or great philosophers of the past? Do you take your cue from pop culture? Do you bring together common beliefs from the major religions of the world? Most of us, when we think about God, start with ourselves.

An old adage reads, "God created man in His own image; man has been returning the favor ever since." That statement has a nugget of truth to it. Our pride has tricked us into believing that we are the center of the universe. The sun and the planets revolve around us, and all that really matters is what we think, feel, and believe. We are the starting point for everything, including God. Consequently, in most discussions about God, we assume ourselves to be at the center. We look around at what we like and dislike, or what we deem to be good and bad, and we transfer our opinions onto God Himself.

But we aren't the starting point in the discussion of the Almighty, because God is not like us. In fact, God is not like anything. He's completely unique in all of the cosmos, and if we want to know what He's like, we must look to Him without any preconceived notions.

That's extraordinarily difficult to do, especially since every person who has walked on the planet has an opinion about God. Whether you believe He exists or not, you still have thoughts about Him. And that's all theology really is—thinking about God.

When we hear God called "holy" and "Father," or we read descriptions of His glory, love, and justice, our lives should change in response to what these terms reveal about His nature. But we can't be affected by the character of God unless we know what those words mean—what they're *really* saying about Him and our relationship to Him.

Let's come to God asking Him who He is, not assuming we already know and not making Him fit the image of who we want Him to be. Easier said than done, right?

1.1 HOLY

"Holy cow." "Holy smokes." "Holy moly."

Exclamations like these are the context in which many of us use the word "holy." The three expressions above are relatively tame, but people have been known to couple many an inappropriate word with "holy," too. I'm sure you've heard a few. Everyone seems to have their own take on Robin's characteristic expression in the "Batman" TV series: "Holy fate worse than death, Batman!"[1]

In the church, we fare a little better. As Christ-followers, the word "holy" often comes to mind when we think about God, and it should. Holiness is a good place to start when considering exactly who God is.

STRENGTH IN NUMBERS

If we take a look at Isaiah 6, for example, we find that beginning to understand holiness is a starting point in learning about God. "Holy" is the cry that is even now ringing in the heavens to describe Him. That's what Isaiah encountered as he was taken up in a vision and saw the Lord:

> "In the year that King Uzziah died, I saw the Lord seated on a high and lofty throne, and His robe filled the temple. Seraphim were standing above Him; each one had six wings: with two he covered his face, with two he covered his feet, and with two he flew. And one called to another:
>
> 'Holy, holy, holy is the LORD of Hosts; His glory fills the whole earth'" (Isaiah 6:1-3).[2]

Can you imagine the scene? Let's not miss the significance that Isaiah "saw the Lord." That alone is amazing, since Isaiah and his people firmly believed it was impossible to see God and live. Even Moses, who we must acknowledge was a guy on intimate terms with God, only saw the back of the Lord as He passed by.[3] But there was Isaiah, taken into God's throne room in heaven, standing face to face with the Almighty.

The creatures attending to God in the throne room had a very distinct call. Their words echoed through the halls of eternity, "Holy, holy, holy." They called out to one another, declaring the holiness of the Lord. In Hebrew, the number three is significant in that it bears the connotation of wholeness. Three signifies that which is real and perfect. It's the number of the Divine. The Trinity exists in three persons: the Father, the Son, and the Holy Spirit. When God appeared to Abraham in Genesis 18, He did so as three strangers. There are three parts to the classic divine blessing of Numbers 6:22-27. "Three" signifies importance and completeness.

---

 1. Burt Ward, who played Robin in the 1960s TV series, had a recurring cameo spot on "Pro Wrestling Unplugged."

 2. *Seraphim* are a type of winged angel. The name literally means "the burning ones."

 3. Read about Moses seeing God's back in Exodus 33:19-23.

By calling God "holy" three times, the seraphim were pointing to the absolutely essential and foundational nature of God's holiness. They didn't chant "loving, loving, loving" or even "glorious, glorious, glorious." They opted for "holy." Therefore, in order to understand a bit of who God is, we must start with this characteristic.

SET APART

To be "holy" is to be separate. Other. Set apart. The word sums up everything that makes God who He is—unique from everything and everyone else. Furthermore, because this is more than just a characteristic of God but rather a summation of all His characteristics, His holiness filters down into everything else we say about Him. God's love is a holy love. His justice is a holy justice. His wrath is a holy wrath. God's holiness reminds us that He is completely and perfectly pure, without spot or blemish. That's part of what John meant when He described God in this way:

> **"Now this is the message we have heard from Him and declare to you: God is light, and there is absolutely no darkness in Him" (1 John 1:5).**

He's not *partly* light just as He's not *partly* holy.

God is wholly "other" than we are. That has big implications for us, because God is very serious about His holiness. We know this is true from a number of places in Scripture, but consider for a minute the manner in which God outlined the building of the tabernacle in the Old Testament. When He delivered the children of Israel from their bondage in Egypt, He had (and still has) a desire to dwell in the midst of His people. But because of His holiness, a certain system was put in place whereby people might appropriately approach Him.

Starting in Exodus 25, Moses dedicated six chapters to the incredibly specific and meticulous way the tabernacle was to be constructed.[4] We read the detailed instructions of how only the high priest could enter the innermost room of the tabernacle and be in the presence of God, and how even the priest was only allowed in on a certain day each year.[5] We also read that in order to come into the presence of a holy God, the priest was required to wear holy garments, have a holy attitude, and have his sin atoned for beforehand.

Why these extreme measures? Why the scores of monotonous verses about the structure of the temple? Why the specifications regarding priestly underwear? It's not because God is a stick-in-the-mud. It's because He is so holy—so other—that His holiness is very, very restrictive. One didn't just barge into the presence of God. There was a protocol to be followed, if not out of reverence, then out of self-preservation.

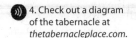 4. Check out a diagram of the tabernacle at *thetabernacleplace.com.*

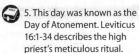 5. This day was known as the Day of Atonement. Leviticus 16:1-34 describes the high priest's meticulous ritual.

THE SEVERITY OF HOLINESS

But beyond that, another story demonstrates God's commitment to His holiness. Second Samuel 6 records the unfortunate story of a guy named Uzzah. The ark of the covenant, the ultimate symbol of God's presence with His people, had been lost in a battle to the Philistines. The Israelites later triumphed in another battle against the Philistines. After the victory, David, Israel's new king, wanted to bring the ark back to its rightful resting place amidst the people of God.

A party atmosphere surrounded the entourage as they began to move the ark. Among the dancers, musicians, and revelry was Uzzah. According to the story, the ark of God was riding on an ox cart when it hit a bumpy place on the road. Uzzah, no doubt with the best of intentions, reached out his hand in order to make sure the ark didn't fall to the ground.

He was struck dead. Instantly.[6]

David was angry. The people were shocked. The ark remained where it was for an extended period of time. And we, like the rest of the crowd, might look at what happened and conclude that God flew off the handle a little bit. After all, Uzzah wasn't trying to desecrate the ark. If anything, he was trying to protect it. But God had instructed the people not to touch the ark, and a holy God means what He says. Uzzah disobeyed, and God rewarded him with death.

Our reaction to that story puts into sharp focus how we treat the holiness of God with little regard. In an over-churched, over-marketed, and over-saturated Christian subculture, is it possible that we've become too familiar with the holy? Are we too comfortable with things we were never meant to be comfortable with?[7]

We would do well to consider how we approach the presence of God. He's the same God who struck down Uzzah and designed the temple with all of its boundaries. He's the God whose holiness is chanted about from the Seraphim even as we speak. Let's heed the advice found in Ecclesiastes 5:1-2:

> **"Guard your step when you go to the house of God. Better to draw near in obedience than to offer the sacrifice as fools do, for they are ignorant and do wrong. Do not be hasty to speak, and do not be impulsive to make a speech before God. God is in heaven and you are on earth, so let your words be few."**

---

 6. The Nazis' faces melted after the ark popped open in *Raiders of the Lost Ark*. That's a picture of the power of God's holiness.

 7. R. C. Sproul has an extensive treatment on the subject in his book *The Holiness of God* if you're looking for more info.

READ. THINK. DISCUSS.

What would you say if someone asked you what it means that God is "holy"?

How often do you think about the holiness of God? Why?

Do you think you might be too familiar with the things of God? Why?

Why do you think God is so serious about His holiness?

What is the proper response for Christ-followers in light of the holiness of God?

Spend time journaling your thoughts
and answers to the questions
that accompany each section.

1.2 GLORY

"To God be the glory, great things He hath done . . ."[8] And so begins an old song sung in many church contexts. Like the song says, God receives glory, and this glory comes from everything from people (i.e. 2 Peter 3:18) to rocks (Luke 19:37-40) to the angels (Luke 2:13-14).[9]

At first glance toward the subject of glory, we would likely be all nods and grins. Of course God deserves the glory from everything He created. He's our Initiator and Sustainer, so He should get the credit He deserves. And in a sense, that's what glory is—recognition, honor, and respect.[10]

Pick any action, person, structure, artistic expression, or element of creation within the entire universe, and you are forced to recognize God as the Source. It's true that there are great painters and song writers, but God is the One who endowed them with their gifts. There are marvelous architects and mavens of business, but God gave them their resources. There are athletes with incredible physical prowess, but it's God who designed their bodies for speed and athletic ability. Even the atheists who curse the name of God as a fabrication and crutch for the weak-minded only do so with the breath God Himself puts in their lungs on a moment-by-moment basis.

GOD'S GLORY IN SCRIPTURE

It's no wonder, then, that the pages of Scripture are replete with acknowledgments of the glory of God and exhortations to give Him that glory. The glory of God is the subject of the second half of the song of the Seraphim in Isaiah 6:3:

> **"Holy, holy, holy is the Lord of Hosts; His glory fills the whole earth."**

The writings of prophets like Habakkuk reveal a longing for the world to be filled with God's glory (Habakkuk 3:2). We see God's refusal to share His glory or praise with the likes of idols in passages like Isaiah 42:8. But God's glory wasn't just something people talked about in Bible times—it was a tangible reality in certain sections of the Old Testament.

God's glory was like a white-hot, consuming fire on top of the mountain when the Lord gave Moses the Ten Commandments (Exodus 24:17). Moses was hidden in the cleft of a rock as the glory of the Lord passed by Him (Exodus 33:22). The glory of the Lord consumed the sacrifice and filled the tabernacle when it was completed (Leviticus 9:23-24). Moments like these left no doubt that God, in all His glory, was among His people.

------

 8. "To God Be the Glory" was written by Frances Crosby. She was blind from six weeks old.

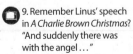 9. Remember Linus' speech in *A Charlie Brown Christmas?* "And suddenly there was with the angel . . . "

 10. The Hebrew word for *glory* means "heavy."

TO GOD BE THE GLORY

God's glory is the source of the praise and honor He deserves. Next to holiness, it's the second characteristic that makes Him unique. God is glorious, but let's not stop there. The Bible doesn't just talk about revelations of God's glory; it firmly establishes the fact that *God seeks His own glory*. That's when it gets a little messy.

It's interesting to flip through the pages of Scripture and notice how often the phrase "to the glory of God" shows up.[11] We typically associate giving ourselves glory with being arrogant, so it's a little uncomfortable to think about God seeking His own glory. But Scripture makes it clear that God's glory is at the heart of His actions, even when people like you and me benefit from those actions (1 Samuel 12:22; Isaiah 43:21; 1 Peter 2:9).

Let's say that you're in great need. Maybe you're sick, or you've lost a job, or you can't seem to do anything right as a parent. You call out to God for help, and He answers. The job comes. Or the healing. Or the wisdom. And you are certainly the beneficiary in that situation. But look more closely and you'll see that your benefit is not the highest reality at work in the situation. Psalm 50:15 says,

> **"Call on Me in a day of trouble; I will rescue you, and you will honor Me."**

Do you see it? We get the deliverance, but God gets the honor. God desires to help us for sure, but His desire is motivated by the glory He will receive. Perhaps the greatest example of this principle at work comes through the act of salvation and the transformation that happens when we cease to be headed for hell and start heading toward heaven.

CENTER OF THE UNIVERSE

Ephesians 1 has a great deal to say about salvation. Verses 3-14 of that chapter describe "every spiritual blessing" we've been given in Christ, including that God has "predestined us to be adopted" and that our inheritance in Christ is absolutely sure and sealed. That's not a bad deal for us, if you ask me. Interestingly enough, those 12 verses, which are so stacked with benefits for us, contain the phrase "to the praise of His glory" three different times. We are saved, but we are saved for the glory of God. We get the benefit of salvation, but God gets the glory for making it happen.

And that's pretty tough to swallow. There are a couple of reasons why we struggle with this truth. The first one, if we're honest, is that we don't like the thought that we aren't the center of God's universe.

I preached for the first time when I was 16 years old. I remember building the entire talk around the TV show "Gilligan's Island," making some veiled references to how we

---

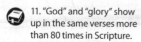
11. "God" and "glory" show up in the same verses more than 80 times in Scripture.

sometimes get stuck on an island and respond, in a spiritual fashion, like the characters on that show. Then later I went back and worked in some Bible references on top of the illustration to make it work. I got lots of compliments and handshakes because I could string a few sentences together.

Armed with that confidence, I went to seminary and was shocked to learn that my professors weren't eagerly anticipating my arrival. In fact, I was even more surprised that there were literally hundreds of students just like me who had clever illustrations and very little knowledge of the Bible. Turns out a lot of people offer the world very similar things to what I offer it. Realizing you're not the center of the universe is an incredibly disillusioning feeling.

We don't like not being the center of the universe. We also don't like those people who haven't realized that the world doesn't revolve around them either. That's the other reason we struggle with God seeking His own glory. Everybody knows *that person* in their lives—the glory hound. The self-centered one who thinks the world revolves around him or her. We know—and don't like—that person. If everything He does is for His own glory, is that what God is like?

GIVING GOD HIS DUE

That was the question of the great Christian author and theologian C. S. Lewis. Before he converted to Christianity, Lewis was well-acquainted with Christian doctrine. He knew that the Bible was said to be the Word of God, as if God Himself had written it. That became a problem for Lewis when he read the Psalms, which contain so many statements about the worship and praise of God. You can't get through five lines in the Psalms without a "praise the LORD" or a "give thanks to the LORD." Lewis reasoned rightly that if this was the inspired Word of God, then God spent a lot of time saying over and over again: "Praise me! Praise me! Praise me!" And to him, that sort of God sounded insecure and weak. In his words, "like a vain woman who wants compliments."[12]

And Lewis would have been right, except for one detail that he later came to realize. It's wrong for anyone or anything else in the universe to command praise of itself, because nothing deserves that praise. Nothing, that is, except God. He's right to demand the praise and glory of the universe because it rightfully belongs to Him. Not only is He right to do it, but demanding glory is an expression of His love. Here's what I mean:

When we truly love someone, we want the best for that person, regardless of whether the best is painful for us or not. And whether we realize it or not, the best thing in the universe isn't family, friends, or money. The best thing in the universe is God. Are you seeing the link?

---

12. C. S. Lewis, *Reflections on the Psalms* (New York: Harcourt, Brace and World, 1958), 94-95.

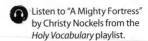 Listen to "A Mighty Fortress" by Christy Nockels from the *Holy Vocabulary* playlist.

If the definition of love is wanting the absolute best for someone (and God is the best in the universe), then for God to truly love us, He must command us to worship and glorify Him. To do anything less would mean He didn't love us at all. In this way, God's jealousy for His name is absolutely inseparable from His love for you and me. As John Piper puts it, "If He is truly for us He must be for Himself!"[13]

Those who believe in the God of the Bible are tasked with glorifying Him. For God's part, He is "jealous" of that glory, demanding it from His people. Paul put it very succinctly in 1 Corinthians 10:31:

> "Therefore, whether you eat or drink, or whatever you do, do everything for God's glory."

In other words, every ounce of your being and every action you do should bring God honor for His role in initiating those things. The glory of God is the ultimate end of our existence. It's what all history points toward. The glory of God (and more specifically, of Jesus) is our destiny:

> "So that at the name of Jesus every knee should bow—of those who are in heaven and on earth and under the earth—and every tongue should confess that Jesus Christ is Lord, to the glory of God the Father" (Philippians 2:10-11).

READ. THINK. DISCUSS.

What would you say if someone asked you to describe God's "glory"?

Why is God's pursuit of His own glory also an act of love toward you and me?

How would your life look different if you were as committed to the glory of God as He is?

What would life be like if you were truly "God-centered"?

What are some practical ways you can become more God-centered this week?

13. John Piper, *Desiring God* (Colorado Springs: Multnomah Publishers, Inc., 2003), 49.

1.3 LOVE

I love my children. I love my wife. But then again, I also love hot dogs. I love a good steak. I love to go to the movies, and I love to read children's fiction. When you stop and think about it, the variety of ways we use the word "love" are quite astounding.

As a culture, we are in love with being in love. We love everything—food, pets, Hollywood personalities, family, and friends. And for Christians, Jesus is on the list of who and what we love, too. I suppose you could argue that our obsession with love might even be good, given the importance placed on the word in Scripture.

THE EPITOME OF LOVE

In John 13:35, Jesus reminded us that we will be able to authenticate our relationship to Him by our love. At another time, He claimed that love was the essence of all the commandments—love of God and love of those around us (Matthew 22:36-39). And when Paul described the greatest characteristics of those who follow Christ, He settled on these three: faith, hope, and love. But then he acknowledged that the greatest of the great is love (1 Corinthians 13:13). To put an exclamation point at the end of things, John—who history would come to know as the beloved disciple—pointed out that those who don't love can't possibly know God, for "God *is* love" (1 John 4:8, emphasis added).

God isn't just loving. He *is* love. And there's a big difference between those two things. A little illustration might help make this point.

The cast of the late '70s and '80s TV show "Happy Days" included a character named Arthur Fonzarelli, aka The Fonz.[14] The Fonz established hair combing and leather jackets as cultural standards. Ask anyone who has seen the show whether or not The Fonz was cool, and you'll get an affirmative yes as they recall his pounding on a jukebox or snapping his fingers. But he didn't just do cool things; he was the epitome of cool, and his coolness seeped into everything he did. Do you see the difference?

At that time, there wasn't a preset definition of cool. You didn't look at the actions of The Fonz, compare those actions to the "cool grid," and then see if his actions fit in. The Fonz was the definition—the starting point—of cool. Something was cool because he did it. Such is the case with God's love.

When God acts in a way that looks like our definition of "loving," we apply the term to Him and say that God is *doing* loving things. When we do this, however, we're guilty of assuming that at other times He may be acting in a way that isn't loving at all. But remember, love is the essence of God's being, so that's simply not possible.

....

 14. *Entertainment Weekly* (*ew.com*) named actor Henry Winkler number 32 on the list of the 100 greatest TV icons of all time for his portrayal of Arthur Fonzarelli.

Any attempt to define love apart from God is a misrepresentation or distortion of what true love is. When we begin to understand this, it becomes clear that when we talk about "love" and when the Bible talks about "the love of God," there are two very different ideas in play.

OUR LOVE VERSUS GOD'S

When we say "love," we generally mean that we like the way something makes us feel. That's true regardless of whether we're talking about a hot dog, a pet, or a person. It's easiest to see that attitude clearly when it comes to food. We love ice cream rather than asparagus, but not because of the nutritional value or the color. We love one and hate the other for one reason and one reason alone: taste.

Is that really so different a definition of love than the one we apply to people? Don't we love those who appeal to us—those who love us in return, who listen to us gripe about our circumstances, and who build up our egos? People like that are easy on the emotional palette, and so we love them.

But God? Well, His love is much different. There are actually several Greek words that are all translated in English to the word "love."[15] Only one Greek word is used in conjunction with God's love, however, and it is *agape*. The interesting thing about the definition of this word is its focus.

When we use the word "love," it's often based on what we get out of the deal. *Agape*, on the other hand, is benevolent love.[16] It is focused on the need of the object of the love. God's love is about what people need, regardless of how they feel about Him at the time.

Probably the most clear example of this love is expressed in Romans 5:6-8:

> **"For while we were still helpless, at the appointed moment, Christ died for the ungodly. For rarely will someone die for a just person—though for a good person perhaps someone might even dare to die. But God proves His own love for us in that while we were still sinners Christ died for us!"**

This passage has much to say about the nature of *agape* love. Notice that the love of God came to us "while we were still sinners." God didn't wait for humanity to clean up its act or become more acceptable to Him. His love wasn't dependent on the goodness of its object; rather, He loved despite our goodness (or lack thereof).

Earlier in the same chapter, in Romans 5:1, Paul wrote that because of Jesus "we have peace with God." If we unpack that statement a little more fully, it means that apart

 15. Listen to C. S. Lewis define the four Greek terms in the audio clip, "Agape Love," on *cslewis.drzeus.net.*

 16. "Agape ... regardless of the object to which it is directed, is participation in the life of God." –Anders Nygren[i]

from the cross we were at war with God. We were His enemies, regardless of whether we recognized it or not. But this is the nature of God's love—it is extended to His enemies, those who hate Him and want nothing to do with His kingdom.

Notice, too, that the love in question isn't theoretical. God didn't sit distantly on His heavenly throne and shout down at humanity through a cosmic megaphone, "I love you! I love you! I love you!" God's love is proven. It's demonstrated. It's a historical reality. We need not question the extent of God's love because He hasn't left any doubt.

How much and to what extent does God love us? The answer is found in two beams and three nails.

ACCEPT AND ENJOY IT

It is impossible, at least from a biblical perspective, to talk about the love of God separate from the crucifixion of Jesus. Every time Paul wrote in his letters about God's love for us, it seems he did so with the cross in the back of his mind. The two are absolutely inseparable, and they should be. The cross is the very definition of love:

> **"Love consists in this: not that we loved God, but that He loved us and sent His Son to be the propitiation for our sins" (1 John 4:10).**

Unfortunately, we are often taught to look upon the cross with guilt and shame because of the role our sinful nature played in putting Jesus there. But that couldn't be a more inappropriate response. The cross was a provisionary and self-sacrificing act; one in which God, in His benevolence, met our deepest need. This makes the cross the standard of God's love.

All that's required of us is the faith to believe that God is love, and yet we struggle to do so. Perhaps we have a hard time believing this truth because no other relationship in our lives is one in which love is so freely and liberally given with no expectations in return. We don't know love this pure or true, so instead of truly accepting and internalizing it, we try continually to earn God's affection.

In so doing, we trivialize the nature of God's lavish love for us. When we separate our notions of love from His, we begin to understand that His love is in no way affected by whether or not we deserve it. Then we feel the freedom to accept His love and rest in it.

Real love isn't meant to be earned; it's meant to be accepted and enjoyed.

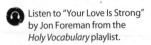

Listen to "Your Love Is Strong" by Jon Foreman from the *Holy Vocabulary* playlist.

READ. THINK. DISCUSS.

Do you think most Christ-followers truly understand the love of God? Why or why not?

How is the way in which you have been loved in the past different from the way God loves you?

How vital to the Christian life is being certain of God's love? Why?

What are some reasons we might have trouble fully believing or accepting the love of God?

1.4 JUSTICE

It would be very difficult to find a more popular word these days than "justice." It's a red-hot term being thrown around by animal rights activists, abolitionists, vegetarians, NRA members, and politicians. And also Christians.

All these groups are clamoring for justice for a variety of people and causes: widows, orphans, victims of abuse, impoverished nations, animals, the unborn, and regular people who have somehow been wronged by someone else. It's safe to say that we, as a culture, like justice . . . at least in concept.

We can be sure that as committed as any of us might be to justice, God is more so. He is the biggest advocate for what's just, despite the best efforts of groups like PETA, the United Nations, the Salvation Army, or the Red Cross. But just like God's love looks completely different from ours, so does His justice, and it's admittedly a challenge to wrap our heads around this characteristic of God.

GOD'S KIND OF JUSTICE

At its most basic definition, justice is the task of upholding moral rightness. The Hebrew word for justice is *mishpat*, and it has to do with the exercise of power and authority. More than 200 times in the Old Testament, the word is used specifically with cases of litigation. To better understand God's justice, it might help us to think about it in terms of a court.

We would hope that one of the defining characteristics of any judge is that he or she is just—that a judge sits on the bench without any impartiality.[17] He or she is there to hear the facts of the case, and to use his or her power to make the right decision. A just judge is able to remove any prejudice he or she might have toward one party or another and make sure that people get exactly what they deserve. Indeed, in a perfectly just world, that would be the standard: Everyone gets exactly what they deserve.

But that's a problematic definition, because who's to say what one person deserves and another person doesn't? By what standard do we measure what people deserve? And is there anyone who can really sit in that seat of judgment without corruption and dispense decisions in a completely fair way? Told you this whole justice thing is complicated.

Typically, when we say we want justice, what we really mean is that we wish things were better for someone, either ourselves or someone else. Our desire for justice is birthed by our perception that things in our lives or the world are unfair. Because we sense unfairness, we want the opposite. That's what we mean when we talk about justice.

---

 17. A common symbol for international court systems is a scale, which depicts balance and equality.

 Check out Kevin DeYoung's blog series "Seven Passages on Social Justice," on *thegospelcoalition.org*.

God, on the other hand, is actually qualified not only to dispense justice, but to define what moral rightness really is. He's not swayed by public opinion. He sits as judge over heaven and earth. And what He says, goes. The Bible makes this absolutely clear with more than 2,000 verses that testify to God's commitment to justice.

God consistently declared Himself to be a friend to the widow and the orphan, a defender of the defenseless. He spoke in straightforward fashion in Isaiah 61:8 that He is a God who loves justice. In the same book, God unleashed a verbal barrage against His people who were acting very religious and yet showed a stark lack of commitment to those in need:

> "Isn't the fast I choose: To break the chains of wickedness, to untie the ropes of the yoke, to set the oppressed free, and to tear off every yoke? Is it not to share your bread with the hungry, to bring the poor and homeless into your house, to clothe the naked when you see him, and to not ignore your own flesh and blood?" (Isaiah 58:6-7).

Because He is a God of justice, He summed up the right response of His people in Micah 6:8:

> "He has told you men what is good and what it is the Lord requires of you: Only to act justly, to love faithfulness, and to walk humbly with your God."

If we need any further proof of God's commitment and love for justice, just take a look at Luke 4. Jesus went back to His hometown of Nazareth. The priest stepped aside and handed Jesus the scroll of Scripture to pick a passage and read. And what did Jesus turn to?

> "He found the place where it was written: 'The Spirit of the Lord is on Me, because He has anointed Me to preach good news to the poor. He has sent Me to proclaim freedom to the captives and recovery of sight to the blind, to set free the oppressed, to proclaim the year of the Lord's favor'" (Luke 4:17-19).

WHERE'S THE JUSTICE?

But if God loves justice so much, and He's qualified to determine and dispense that justice, how do we explain the incredible amount of human suffering in the world? How do we reconcile this great lover of justice with the millions of starving orphans? With the enormous sex trade? With the radically uneven distribution of income across the world? Are these evidences of God's justice?

The answer is no. The issues in the preceding questions aren't examples of justice; they're just a few of the world's injustices. And rest assured about this: The Lord is angry

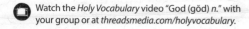 Watch the *Holy Vocabulary* video "God (gŏd) *n.*" with your group or at *threadsmedia.com/holyvocabulary*.

about them. But they do remind us that any discussion about true justice can't be had outside of eternity. We are limited by space and time; we only see the realities of our present, and what we know to be true of the past.

God, on the other hand, doesn't have the same limitations.[18] The divine commitment to justice goes well beyond the confines of this earth. It extends into the far reaches of forever and into the realm where the will of God is done fully and completely. To God, there is no past, present, or future. There is only now. And what that means related to justice is that every evil perpetrated in the history of humanity still stinks in the nostrils of the divine. God doesn't "get over" anything.

We might be tempted, in light of that fact, to simply turn our heads at injustice in the world. *After all,* we might reason, *God's going to drop the hammer on judgment day. Let's just let justice take hold then.* If we choose that option, we are most likely masking our selfishness and desire for comfort with conviction. We don't want to be inconvenienced by thinking or doing anything about the state of the world, so we use God as an excuse for our laziness.[19] But that's not what we're called to do.

WE MUST BE INVOLVED

Take a look back at Isaiah 58. It seems that the people were very good at being religious. They were great at praying, fasting, and generally looking rather serious and grave. And yet God was angry, because in all of their religiosity, their neighbors were going hungry. Their countrymen were without homes. Their family members were outside in the cold. God's response was simple: "Really? Really? You really think you're impressing Me by skipping a few meals?"

With the same words, God cuts to the core of much of our religious commitment. For us, as for those Israelites, our faith is largely about personal commitment. And truth be told, we're pretty good at it. But through the haze of personal discipline comes the voice of God reminding us, "It's great that you've only eaten chicken broth for four days. How about that guy on the street corner? He's pretty hungry. Maybe you could give some of those meals you're skipping to him."

We must learn to love justice the way God loves justice. We must commit ourselves to bringing about God's standards here on the earth. That may seem like an impossible task—and one that won't be completed until evil is erased and we're in eternity—but it's a big part of our role as Christ-followers.

Pursuing God's justice now is part of preparing for the coming kingdom of God. That includes accepting the facts that what we deem "fair" may not always be the case, and justice isn't always going to work out in our favor. We also ought to be careful what we

---

 18. Read Mark Buchanan's *Things Unseen* for thoughts beyond our limited perspective.

 19. "If we claim affinity for Christ but turn a blind eye to those He identified Himself with, there is no honor in that." –Jen Hatmaker[ii]

SESSION ONE HOLY VOCABULARY

wish for, so that we don't ask God for justice when what we really want is convenience and comfort. I have a feeling God's justice looks little like the American Dream.

READ. THINK. DISCUSS.

If you were suddenly treated in a completely just fashion, how would your life change?

How does your own commitment to justice stack up against God's? Why?

Why do you think God is so passionate about justice?

Do you feel that most churches mirror God's commitment and love for justice? Why or why not?

What are some ways you might begin to pursue justice in your everyday life?

1.5 FATHER

Few words carry as much baggage as the title "father." Ask people about their fathers and you'll get a range of responses from "my hero" to "the reason I'm so messed up." No wonder the characteristic of God's fatherhood is such a touchy and difficult subject for us to embrace.

Though we're meant to take great comfort from the privilege of calling God our Father, the name has the opposite effect for many. When some people think of a father, they may think of absence instead of intimacy. Even worse, some may think of a man who abused his role and corrupted their notion of what a father is really supposed to be. If that's the case with you, then in order to accept God's role as your Father, you have to learn what a father *is supposed to do.*

A perfect father cares, protects, encourages, and advises. But above all, he loves. Always and without condition. A perfect father waits on the porch to welcome home his children regardless of where they've been or what they've done. A perfect father is proud of his children and takes no greater pleasure in the world than giving them what they need.

No matter how close anyone's dad comes to being perfect, he'll inevitably fall short of the perfect way God models this relationship.

GOD AS FATHER
"Our Father which art in heaven . . ."

Those are familiar words. It's the beginning line of what has become known as "The Lord's Prayer."[20] In modern usage, this prayer has become something of an incantation, recited laboriously before a sports event or a civic meeting. It's become a tool we use in an attempt to guarantee God's endorsement of whatever we're about to do. However, the verses immediately preceding the prayer are a warning against the kind of praying that amounts to mindless repetition (Matthew 6:5-8).

A better description for this prayer might be "The Model Prayer," since Jesus never meant for His specific prayer to be repeated over and over again. Jesus advised that His followers pray like this—not pray exactly this. In praying like Jesus, the starting point for how we approach God as Christ-followers is summed up in this single word: Father.

To hear Jesus speak like that must have been shocking for the folks sitting on the hillside that day.[21] Oh, He'd warmed them up with His controversial statements about what it really means to be called "blessed" and His proclamation that thinking badly of someone is the same as killing them. But the introduction of the word "Father" took the sermon to another level.

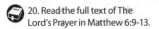

20. Read the full text of The Lord's Prayer in Matthew 6:9-13.

21. The Model Prayer is found in the Sermon on the Mount (Matthew 5–7), Jesus' most extensive teaching on record.

Judaism held strongly to the belief that God was absolutely unapproachable. Was He to be loved? Sure. Respected? Absolutely. Feared? Without question. This was the culture that wouldn't even speak God's name, and when they had to write it in Scripture, they did so with great honor and respect. Some traditions say the scribes would break the pens they used to write the name after they were finished to guarantee the same pen wouldn't later be used to blaspheme God.[22]

Enter Jesus, this strange Rabbi who had no fear or regard for the religious leaders of the time and who spoke with unmatched authority. There He was on a hillside talking about the revered God of Israel with an air of unmistakable familiarity. That level of familiarity was just what God intended. It's not that God wanted to be disrespected or approached casually; far from it. God wanted to be in a relationship with His people that was marked by love rather than fear. One impacted by an appreciation of His great grace and compassion, rather than apprehension toward Him. He wanted to be their dad.

HIS SONS AND DAUGHTERS

We see God's love most tangibly in this father-child relationship. John described it like this in 1 John 3:1:

> **"Look at how great a love the Father has given us, that we should be called God's children."**

God's great love doesn't make us His servants. It doesn't make us the people He puts up with. God's great love makes us His sons and daughters. In his letter to the Ephesians, Paul uses the imagery of adoption to describe the Christian's place as a child of God:

> **"In love He predestined us to be *adopted* through Jesus Christ for Himself, according to His favor and will, to the praise of His glorious grace that He favored us with in the Beloved" (Ephesians 1:4-6, emphasis added).**

God has such an intense desire for fatherhood that He's willing to adopt spiritual orphans out of the world into His family. As God's adopted children, we become coheirs with Jesus in God's blessings that await us in heaven.[23] In a sense, we've been brought into God's house from the cold outdoors, never to be thrown out again. That's what a perfect Father does.

God is committed to making sure we understand the nature of the relationship we can have with Him. In fact, He wants us to know Him as Father so much that one of the primary functions of the Holy Spirit is to remind us of His closeness:

> **"All those led by God's Spirit are God's sons. For you did not receive a spirit of slavery to fall back into fear, but you received the Spirit of adoption, by**

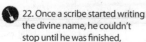
22. Once a scribe started writing the divine name, he couldn't stop until he was finished, even to greet the king.

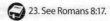
23. See Romans 8:17.

whom we cry out, 'Abba, Father!' The Spirit Himself testifies together with our spirit that we are God's children" (Romans 8:14-16).[24]

The Holy Spirit of God lives inside of us for many reasons, but a big part of His role is to remind us of our true identity. He's there to whisper over and over in our ears, "You are a child of God. He is your Father." And let's be honest, we need that reminder, because like all adopted children, we have a certain amount of trauma in our past. Though much of our trauma is self-inflicted—since we've all made our fair share of bad choices—we're nevertheless abused, neglected, and worn out.

Psychologists advise new adopting parents that one of the greatest things they can do for their children is to make them feel safe and remind them that they aren't going to be put out or forsaken.[25] God is very concerned that we, too, know we aren't going to be put out. We're safe and secure.

Another reason we need to be reminded of God's fatherhood is because of the overwhelming temptation for us to look at our circumstances and doubt whether or not He really is our Father at all. We're people who struggle financially. We undergo chemotherapy. We can't seem to overcome sin. We're the tired, the poor, and the unfaithful, and because we are, we tend to forget that God is our Father.

So the Holy Spirit reminds us, again and again. He reminds us in the midst of our pain and when we try to be self-reliant. He reminds us when we're in the throws of temptation. Time and time again comes the echo of the Spirit in our hearts: *We are children of God.*

DISCIPLINE OF LOVE

When we come upon trouble in this life, our natural inclination is to doubt the love and care of God. We think, *If God really loved me, I wouldn't continue to struggle with [fill in the blank].* Or *If God is supposed to always be there, why do I feel so helpless and alone?* We often look at troubling circumstances as evidence of God's absence, a testimony to His distance.

But nothing could be further from the truth. As the Spirit of Truth, we also rely on the Holy Spirit to re-educate us on what it means for God to be called our Father, and He reminds us that we see evidence of God's fatherhood in our struggles.[26]

The Book of Hebrews tells us that because God is our Father, we can expect Him to operate in a truly fatherly manner. And one of the things a father does is discipline His children:

> "Endure it as discipline: God is dealing with you as sons. For what son is there whom a father does not discipline? But if you are without discipline—which all receive—then you are illegitimate children and not sons" (Hebrews 12:7-8).

---

 24. *Abba* points to the familiarity and intimacy God desires. Think of it as "Daddy."

 25. By law parents can't exclude their adopted children from their wills.

 26. God reminded His church, *"As many as I love, I rebuke and discipline" (Revelation 3:19).*

SESSION ONE HOLY VOCABULARY

Imagine entering a full and hectic childcare room at the local gym. Upon entering the room, it can look a little disconcerting. You may find children with their clothes on backwards, with objects sticking out of their noses, and throwing various degrees of temper tantrums. Those long-suffering workers catch the brunt of everything that's not happening (or is happening) at each child's home.

If we were to ask those childcare workers, "What would make your job a little easier?," my guess is that they might affirm the value and importance of parental discipline at home. "But wait," we might say. "Don't you want those parents to love their kids? How can putting them in time-out, grounding them, or punishing them in some way be loving?" Well, the truth is that discipline is an act of love, not evidence of the lack of it.

The very fact that God loves us enough to discipline us is evidence of His fatherhood. It doesn't mean God is distant or absent. In fact, it's quite the opposite. As with any parent's discipline, God is so involved in our lives that He wants to play a key role in helping us realize our full potential as His children. God's discipline means He cares about us enough to take a very personal interest in our development as children in the faith. Regardless of what you associate with the term "father," this caring, loving, and disciplining One is our perfect Daddy.

READ. THINK. DISCUSS.

How do you think your relationship with your earthly father has influenced what you believe to be true about God, either positively or negatively?

How do you think God feels when His children call Him Father?

What aspects of your spiritual life mirror the closeness of that title? What aspects are furthest away?

In what ways have you experienced God as Father in the past? Were some of them more comfortable than others? How so?

Leading a group? It's the way to go. Find extra questions and teaching tools in the leader kit, available on *threadsmedia.com/holyvocabulary.*

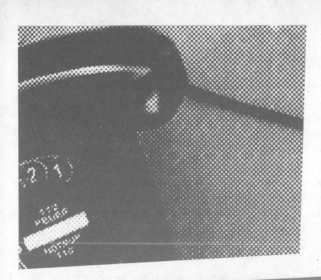

HUMANITY

THE HUMANITY OF US ALL

In 2010 the Hollywood blockbuster *Avatar* became the highest grossing movie of all time. "The Sims" is the best selling computer game of all time. What do these two things have in common? Life simulation. There's a whole subculture out there fascinated with computer-generated altar-egoes, complete with whatever look, personality, and interests you choose. Those things give humanity the chance to taste what it's like to have your world look any way you want it to.

At the root of this phenomenon is the question of identity. Who am I? Why am I here? What control do I have? These are some big questions, but they're the same questions we all ask, gamers or not. Luckily, they're questions about which the Bible has a lot to say.

God didn't breathe life into men and women because He was lonely. We don't exist because He needed someone to confide in. We were made like all children ought to be made—not out of deficiency, but out of an overflow of love. The complete love within the Trinity overflowed in creation, and Adam and Eve found themselves walking in the garden of Eden. We were created to enjoy God in perfect intimacy and fellowship, reflecting His glory into the entire earth. Humans were created in God's image, with the incredible capacity to know and enjoy God. But selfishly, we thought there was something better. And that was our first mistake.

Yes, we've made mistakes. Lots of them. Scripture is quick to point out that humanity is not perfect. Almost from the beginning of the Bible we're confronted with our failures. We find selfishness, greed, and a startling lack of consistency and commitment. We find killers, adulterers, cowards, liars, and thieves. We find the worst in us, yet through it all we find a God who is continually running after His people.

In Christianity, we bring nothing to the table. In fact, the only thing we bring to the salvation equation is the sin we need to be rescued from. But thankfully, gloriously, and amazingly, the Bible doesn't stop with our mistakes. There's great news for humanity. We have an incredible destiny.

In order to truly appreciate who we're becoming, we have to understand who we were and who we are now. We must take a serious look at the words we use to talk about our humanity—words like sin, saved, or believe. It's critical that we understand the ways we talk about ourselves and our relationship to God. Believe me, He's dreamed up something so much better for you than any simulated world you could imagine.

2.1 SIN

Few topics polarize people as much as a discussion about "sin." As a matter of fact, sin is often considered a taboo subject that's off limits or out of bounds. But the world doesn't reject sin because people are convicted about its presence in their lives or are modest in their efforts to overcome it. The world rejects the concept of sin entirely.

According to the dictionary, *sin* is "transgression of divine law; any act regarded as a transgression, especially a willful or deliberate violation of some religious or moral principle."[1] This definition causes friction in a culture like ours, where the philosophical bent is moving increasingly toward a rejection of absolute truth.

SIN IN A TOLERANT SOCIETY

Greater numbers of people are choosing to believe there is no set standard for "good" or "evil." Instead, they believe all ethics are situational—what's considered "good" or "right" for one isn't true for everyone.[2] This system of thought has incredibly far-reaching implications. It means that any action is morally ambiguous. The context of the action must be explored to know if it's really good or bad. Theft, murder, adultery—these actions might be frowned upon, but they can't be declared as universally "wrong" without taking into account the circumstances surrounding the action.

The question now isn't whether an action or belief is right or wrong; it's whether the specific action or belief works for the individual doing or believing it. In the absence of absolute truth, pragmatism is king.

That's a good summation of the way many people look at religion these days. More and more people are ascribing to the view that being a part of a religious system is a lot like climbing a mountain with many pathways.[3] Some people hold the opinion that Christians, Buddhists, Muslims, and so forth, are all on the same mountain trying to ascend to the top, they're just taking different pathways to get there. When they finally reach the top, they find God. Or enlightenment. Or Allah. People who agree with this thought process would argue that it doesn't really matter what you call "god," because he's really the same being. And it doesn't matter what path you're on, since they're all headed to the same place.

If this is a common approach to religion, then no wonder sin is a touchy subject. If we call an action "sinful," we're imposing our personal definition of morality on others. And that imposition is the only thing a tolerant society deems categorically wrong. Such judgment is considered the epitome of arrogance and the mind-set of the unenlightened, outdated, and uneducated.

---

1. From *dictionary.com*.

 2. Sixty-four percent of American adults say truth is relative to the person and their situation (*barna.org*).

 3. One in four Americans dabble in multiple religions, according to a 2009 survey from the Pew Research Center.

SESSION TWO HOLY VOCABULARY

But this tolerant approach to morality simply doesn't square with what it means to follow Christ. Christians must be convinced of the absolute truth of God's law and the reality of sin. If we aren't, then God is only a tool we use to have a better life. If we reject sin, we have no real need for God. But sin *is* real; indeed, sin is the root cause of everything we see wrong with the world today.

WHERE WE WENT WRONG

It all started with the events that unfold in the Book of Genesis. God, out of an overflow of the love between the members of the Trinity, created everything, including men and women. After each creation, whether a fish or an antelope or the Venus fly-trap or Saturn, God remarked that His creation was "good." That pattern changed, though, when He came to the creation of humanity. This outgrowth of God's creative force was not called good; humanity stands alone in the story of creation with the designation of being "very good" (Genesis 1:31).

God created men and women with Himself in mind, and these new people were the bearers of His image. God determined that Adam and Eve, the first humans, were to extend the glory of God on earth by ruling justly and lovingly over creation and under His authority.

In a vivid description of those early days, Genesis records that the first man and woman "were naked, yet felt no shame" (Genesis 2:25). These people had nothing to hide—no moral failings or insecurities. They were completely vulnerable to God and each other. It was, simply, a situation of perfect fellowship. But then everything changed.

A deceiver corrupted the word of God.[4] Humanity believed the lie and chose to live outside the loving rule of its Creator. And suddenly, earth was radically changed. Sin had entered the world. The effect was devastating, and we're still reeling from it.

Vulnerability was replaced with shame. Love was overtaken by fear. Order was dissolved into chaos. The fellowship was broken, and along with it, the rest of the world. The first humans, in their willful disobedience, dug an uncrossable trench between themselves and God. And the rest of creation spiraled downward. Earthquakes, tornadoes, famine, flood—these aren't ultimately the result of weather patterns, environmental changes, or melting ice caps. They're the result of sin:

> **"For we know that the whole creation has been groaning together with labor pains until now" (Romans 8:22).**

ATTACKING SIN AT ITS ROOT

The Greek definition for *sin* is simply "to miss the mark." We were created in the image of

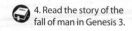 4. Read the story of the fall of man in Genesis 3.

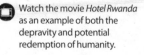 Watch the movie *Hotel Rwanda* as an example of both the depravity and potential redemption of humanity.

God with the intent to glorify Him through our worship and enjoyment of Him forever.[5] But we've missed that mark—big time. We choose to worship money, sex, and other pretend gods rather than the Almighty. We enjoy the menial pleasures of such things as hamburgers when we could enjoy walking with Him each day. We've missed the mark. It's a simple definition for the far-reaching condition in which we find ourselves.

Don't miss the fact that sin isn't so much an action as a condition. It's true, we sin whenever we violate God's revealed will. But we do so because it's in our nature. Let me put it another way—we don't become sinners when we sin; we sin because we're sinners. That's our heritage. It's the spiritual DNA we inherited from the parents of the human race. Understanding that fact is imperative because it radically influences the way we think about the solution to sin.

If sin is merely a bad choice or a set of bad choices, then the solution is easy enough: Quit doing that thing. Just stop. Simple, right?

But if sin is more than just a choice—if sin is a state of being or a condition—then our problems run a lot deeper than just doing the occasional bad thing. In that case, we don't need to "stop sinning" because we can't. Just as apples can't will themselves to be oranges, we can't stop ourselves from sinning. Our natural inclination is toward evil and disobedience. Sure, we might will ourselves to be pretty good citizens, but that doesn't change the inherent condition of our hearts. That initial choice of Adam and Eve plunged us into a reality of darkness from which we can't escape.[6]

That's why the gospel is so much more than an attempt to change our behavior. The gospel is about a change in being. In condition. In who we are. Because sin runs so deeply into the very core of who we are, the solution for sin can be nothing less than an absolute change of that same core.

STRIVING FOR GOD'S STANDARD

Paul left little doubt as to the state of our condition when he wrote this in Romans 3:10-12:

> **"There is no one righteous, not even one; there is no one who understands, there is no one who seeks God. All have turned away, together they have become useless; there is no one who does good, there is not even one."**

Wait a minute, though. Can we really say that for certain? Every day Christians and non-Christians do things that are good—for others, for themselves, and for the planet. There are humanitarian organizations around the world. Surely those people do good and Paul was blowing the situation out of proportion here. Right?

---

 5. The Westminster Shorter Catechism (1648) describes this as "the chief end of man."

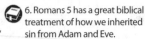 6. Romans 5 has a great biblical treatment of how we inherited sin from Adam and Eve.

Wrong. I'm not trying to say that people aren't doing good things. I'm certainly not trying to devalue any relief or humanitarian efforts around the globe. But perhaps we would do well to examine what our definition of "good" really is. In this situation, we must come back to where we started: Is there an ultimate standard of good in the universe? If so, then anything that detracts from that standard can't be called good. In fact, it's the opposite. God is the ultimate standard of good, and nothing is good apart from Him. He sets the mark that we miss completely. Based on that starting point, we aren't good. Not good at all.

Sin is the answer to the fundamental human question: What's wrong with us?

Thankfully, the story doesn't end with our sinfulness. In fact, everything that happens in the Bible after Genesis 3 describes God's efforts to bring us back to Him, remove our sinfulness, and restore the perfect relationship He had with His creation before sin ever entered the picture.[7] Keep reading.

READ. THINK. DISCUSS.

How often do you think about sin? Why?

How often do you think God wants you to think about it?

What are the top three words that come to mind when you think of sin?

Why is sin such a reprehensible concept for the culture at large?

How should the Christ-follower respond to a cultural viewpoint as described above?

7. There's hope: *"But God proves His own love for us in that while we were still sinners Christ died for us!" (Romans 5:8).*

2.2 LOST

I have the unfortunate claim to fame of having been lost in a great variety of cities and towns across the United States. Orlando? Been lost there. Los Angeles? Been lost there, too. Austin? Oh sure. Memphis? Most definitely. Atlanta? Right on. Oklahoma City? I once spent $30 on the toll road because I couldn't figure out which way to go. Ruston, Louisiana? Yep. This last one is particularly embarrassing since Ruston has a population of approximately 21,000 people. But in my defense, the roads are really curvy.

Being lost is an incredibly frustrating thing. When you're lost, you inevitably find yourself losing other things: time, patience, and self-respect, to name a few. But the worst part of being lost comes in the fateful moment when you pull into a gas station, finally acknowledging that you don't know the way.

It's humiliating. After all, we should know where we're going. We're educated, sophisticated people. We're grown-ups who pay the rent and the TiVo® bill. We're self-reliant, yet when we're lost, we find ourselves standing in front of the beef jerky and slurpies with our hats in our hands begging for help.

Given that, it's no wonder why the word *lost* has fallen on hard times in Christian circles. Nobody likes to be lost, so why would anyone want to be called lost? But for years in the church, the term *lost* is how Christians have described those outside the faith. Unfortunately, there's often a note of condescension in our voices when we talk about the lost world around us. Like a local mocking the lost out-of-towner driving in circles, we as the "found" have a tremendous amount of pride in the fact that we supposedly know the way.

WHO'S LOOKING FOR US?

Lost isn't a bad word; in fact, it's a biblical word. It's a word that can't be separated from the identity of Jesus. The Son of God made it crystal clear that His mission to earth was about the lost:

> **"For the Son of Man has come to seek and to save the lost" (Luke 19:10).**

That statement came in response to Jesus' encounter with a diminutive, tree-climbing scallywag named Zacchaeus.[8] If ever a man was lost, Zacchaeus was that man. He spent his adult life living exclusively for himself. As a tax collector, he was seen as a traitor to his people, the Jews, since he worked for the Roman government. And this man wasn't interested in changing his reputation; the story reveals that he had grown rich from pilfering extra taxes from the common folk. The result was a lonely existence with no friends, no reputation, and certainly no direction in life.[9]

 "I have never been lost, but I will admit to being confused for several weeks." –Daniel Boone[iii]

 8. Interestingly enough, the name *Zacchaeus* means "innocent."

 9. Read the full story of this man in Luke 19:1-10.

In a way, Zacchaeus is a great representation of all humanity. Day by day we wander through life with our primary goal being the pursuit of anything to make us feel whole. Money, sex, power—these are all attempts to complete ourselves, to find our purpose, and to establish who we are. We have no idea why we're here, what we're doing, or where we're headed. Like Zacchaeus, we are lost.

The entrance of sin into the world as recorded in Genesis 3 has incredible implications for the direction of our lives. We noted earlier how sin threw the entire created order into chaos, leaving a rift between man and God. But let's not stop there. Because of sin, we're directionally lost. We have twisted versions of what good, love, justice, hope, and pleasure really are. Our minds and hearts are wandering, confused as to whether down is really up and north is really south.

Look again at Luke 19:10:

> **"For the Son of Man has come to seek and to save the lost."**

In this verse, Luke highlighted two of Jesus' primary roles as the Son of God: Seeker and Savior.[10] In order to save the lost from their sinful natures, Jesus first seeks them out. He did this while on earth, as we saw with Zacchaeus. He also did this with us.

It shouldn't surprise us that Jesus was and is a seeker, because He takes after His Father. In Genesis 3, God walked in the cool of the garden and sought after His first kids. In Ezekiel 22, He looked for someone who would stand on the wall and intercede for the people. Second Chronicles 16 describes Him scanning the earth, looking for one whose heart was fully committed to Him.

Now we must assume there's a difference between our looking for something and God's. When God seeks, He knows what He'll find. His isn't a blind search, looking everywhere; it's much more focused and intentional. So the Father has been looking. Now the Son is looking, too.

I imagine that wherever Jesus went, His eyes were constantly darting back and forth, focused, always looking this way and that. Not in an anxious way, but seeking for specific places and moments to make Himself known. That's the picture of Jesus the looker—the Seeker—that Luke gives us.

You get the sense from reading about the journeys of Jesus that He had a specific destination in mind—the hill with the tree and the nails. That was where He was headed. But if you map out the route He took to get there, it certainly wasn't the most direct one. It was full of twists and turns, back tracking, and moving into obscure villages. Although He was well aware of

---

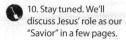 10. Stay tuned. We'll discuss Jesus' role as our "Savior" in a few pages.

His destination, it seems as if He had various appointments along the way—appointments so important that they took Him out of the way, sometimes for days or even months, on His journey to Jerusalem. But that was all part of the looking and searching.

THE JOY OF BEING FOUND

In Luke 15, Jesus told three stories about what it means to be lost. These stories involve a lost sheep, a lost coin, and a lost son.[11]

The coin and the sheep were both helpless and without hope unless someone found them—someone who was willing to go to great personal effort and cost to seek them out. But the most striking part of those parables isn't the degree of lostness. It's the reaction of the seekers once their objects are found. All three stories end in celebration. The shepherd "joyfully" carried his sheep all the way home and called his neighbors to join him in celebrating the sheep that was no longer lost. In the case of the woman and her coin, the celebration far exceeded the actual worth of the coin, and the invited guests probably left wondering why the woman had celebrated so lavishly after finding her money.

But the father took rejoicing over the lost being found to a whole different level. His younger son had asked to be treated as he would if his father were dead. He took his inheritance and squandered it away before he came to his senses and returned home, ashamed of what he'd done. Meanwhile, the father had been sitting on the front porch waiting for his lost son to come home.

When the father finally saw his son approaching in the distance, he ran to meet him. The old man hiked up his robes so they wouldn't tangle his feet and sprinted as fast as his legs could carry him.[12] Can you picture it? With tears in his eyes, he "ran, threw his arms around his neck, and kissed him" (Luke 15:20). He didn't wait for apologies. Overcome with joy, he threw a ridiculously large celebration for him. In fact, the father called for the slaughter of the fattened calf, one that had probably been raised to use specifically for a sacrifice to God.

Being lost is bad, especially when we don't know how lost we are. That was certainly the case of the sheep and the coin, as well as the younger son, initially. They had no idea that they were off track, but despite their lack of awareness, someone found them. Someone looked. Someone ran. And someone celebrated.

Jesus didn't always directly connect His parables to the lives of the people listening. He often left it up to them to draw the connection; but not so with the lost parables. Jesus made the connection to their (and our) lives explicitly clear:

---

 11. Timothy Keller's book *The Prodigal God* contains amazing reflection on the last of these parables.

12. In that day and time, running was extremely undignified.

> "I tell you, in the same way, there will be more joy in heaven over one sinner who
> repents than over 99 righteous people who don't need repentance" (Luke 15:7).

If you look back at the first verse in Luke 15, you see that there were actually a couple types of lost people listening to Jesus that day. There were the obvious lost—the tax collectors and the sinners who were steeped in sin and therefore tried, judged, and convicted by their countrymen. But there was another group.

Standing behind the obvious lost was a group of people who were just as lost (if not more so), except they didn't know it. The religious leaders of the day were complaining about Jesus and His habit of welcoming and eating with "sinners." So Jesus handed out the double whammy of Luke 15. With this series of parables, He revealed the great depth of the lostness of the crowd—both conscious and unconscious lost people.

Which type are we? The ones with need or the ones with pride? The ones with questions or the ones who think we know the answers? Both groups need the Seeker. Just like the shepherd, the woman, and the father, Jesus seeks after the lost, runs to them, and celebrates with us and the angels when they're found. We can't fathom the lengths the great Seeker of souls has gone to in order to find us.

READ. THINK. DISCUSS.

What do you think of when you hear the word "lost"?

What does it mean to be lost in a spiritual sense?

How does it make you feel to know Jesus and the angels celebrated when you were found?

Describe the differences between the characters in the parables who were condescending toward the lost objects or person and those who weren't.

Given God's attitude about the lost, what should our attitude be?

How does remembering your own former lostness change the way you worship and pray?

2.3 REPENT

Now here's a word that belongs on a sandwich board. When we see the word "repent," we immediately think of the crazy street preacher with the scraggly beard who bellows over and over at the top of his lungs, "Repent! The end is near!"

Despite that connotation, the biblical importance of the word cannot be overstated. The prophets demanded repentance during seasons of national sin in the Old Testament.[13] It was the core message of John the Baptist (Matthew 3:2). And it was the response Peter gave on the Day of Pentecost when the people asked him what they should do about the fact that Jesus was crucified and then raised from the dead:

> "'Repent,' Peter said to them, 'and be baptized, each of you, in the name of Jesus the Messiah for the forgiveness of your sins, and you will receive the gift of the Holy Spirit'" (Acts 2:38).

As important as repentance is, it's drastically misunderstood. In our church lingo, *repent* has come to mean nothing more than "stop." Whatever that sinful thing is you're doing—from idol worship to illicit sexual behavior, coarse joking, or gluttony—grit your teeth and quit doing it. But that's not what *repent* means at all, and with that interpretation we miss the love that's an integral part of the biblical mandate.

TURNING, NOT JUST STOPPING

To *repent* means "to turn," not to stop. Turning is a different movement than stopping. It requires more motion and force.[14] You can stop and still be facing the same direction, sitting motionless. And though stopping sinful behavior is important, it's really only the halfway point in the fullness of true repentance. When you don't just stop but turn, you choose to move away from what you were doing and toward something else. Something better. Think of it in terms of a rebound relationship.

I've had one before; maybe you have, too. A rebound relationship is the relationship that happens shortly after another one (one you were really into) ends. You really liked the previous girl/boyfriend, but that relationship is over. And though you might not realize it at the time, your relationship with the next person has more to do with the last relationship than the new one. You like the current person OK, but you're still trying to get over what just happened in your previous relationship. In short, you haven't turned toward the new person; you're still trying to walk away from the old one.

We do that in relationships, but we also do it in other areas of life. When the moment comes that we feel the need to leave a church, we can easily get fixated on leaving. We leave because of this reason or that—preaching or financial decisions or children's education or

---

 13. The 10 days between Rosh Hashanah and Yom Kippur are days devoted to repentance. Read about this in Leviticus 23.

 "You will not despise a broken and humbled heart" (Psalm 51:17).

 14. In physics, stopping is a simple movement, but turning is a complex movement because it requires more force.

whatever. So we walk away, sometimes with hurt feelings and a sense of bitterness. We do it with jobs. We get fed up with policies or managers, or we get bored with our list of tasks. So we walk away, glad to be leaving the drudgery behind.

It happens with sin too. We walk away from sin. We decide to stop a habitual practice of pornography, gossiping, overeating, or anything else destructive. We walk away and leave the ways of the past behind. In all of these cases, our walking away is reactionary. And it's an act of the will—we are choosing to get out of a bad situation, which is a good thing, and a start in the right direction.

But we can only walk away from something for so long. Eventually, just walking away wears us out. We get tired. We get bitter. We get angry. A moment must come when we aren't just walking away from something. At some point, we have to catch a vision, a breath, a taste of something that turns our attention and focus in a new direction. Only then can we truly leave things in the past and get excited about the future.

In order for repentance to hold, for it to "stick," we must be convinced that we're choosing something better than what we're leaving behind. Our motivation has to be *turning toward* something rather than just *walking away* from something else.

Walking away is reactionary.

Turning toward is anticipatory.

Walking away is angry.

Turning toward is hopeful.

Walking away is will.

Turning toward is faith.

TURNING TOWARD SOMETHING BETTER

The "something" we must choose to turn toward is Jesus. C. S. Lewis understood this when he wrote the following in *The Weight of Glory*: "We are half-hearted creatures, fooling about with drink and sex and ambition when infinite joy is offered us, like an ignorant child who wants to go on making mud pies in a slum because he cannot imagine what is meant by the offer of a holiday at the sea. We are far too easily pleased."[15]

According to Lewis (and the Bible for that matter), our problem isn't that we seek too much pleasure; it's that we settle for too little. Over and over again in Scripture, but particularly

---

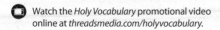 Watch the *Holy Vocabulary* promotional video online at *threadsmedia.com/holyvocabulary*.

15. C. S. Lewis, *The Weight of Glory: and other addresses* (New York: HarperCollins Publishers, 1980), 16.

in the Psalms, we're urged to delight ourselves in the Lord (Psalm 37:4). The psalmist acknowledged that God was his joy (Psalm 43:4), and that in "Your presence is abundant joy; in Your right hand are eternal pleasures" (Psalm 16:11).

Repentance is about choosing life with Christ over life with anything else. So repentance isn't about *stopping* what we're doing; it's about valuing Jesus *more than* what we're doing. That's why we turn; not just because our old ways are self-destructive, wrong, or immoral, but because of how much we value Christ. And how much we believe He's better than anything else.

We see this biblical principle in a number of places in Scripture, but consider the sin of the people recorded in Jeremiah 2:12-13:

> "Be horrified at this, heavens; be shocked and utterly appalled. This is the LORD's declaration. For My people have committed a double evil: They have abandoned Me, the fountain of living water, and dug cisterns for themselves, cracked cisterns that cannot hold water."

What was so horrifying? What was the great sin? The people of Jeremiah's day were content with the tiny, insignificant, temporary pleasures of the world. Instead of pursuing in faith the eternal joy and satisfaction that can only be found in God, they were busy making their mud pies in the stuff of earth. God wanted, and wants, something better for His people.

Foundational to real repentance is the belief that the true treasure and joy of the universe is God alone. It's the rock-solid conviction that when we choose anything above God, we're choosing something less than the best. That's why God doesn't speak out of anger when He says, "Repent." He speaks out of love. He's saying, "You are settling. Don't you want something better?"

Real repentance requires us to recognize the love of God, but it also requires more faith than will. See, I typically try to repent of something by just deciding not to do it anymore. And I try. And then I fail. So I try harder next time. But what I really need to do is exercise the faith it takes to believe that Jesus is actually better than anything else. We choose to believe Jesus is more—He is better. So we turn.

Repentance is at the core of Christianity. The call to repent isn't limited to one specific time and action. Repentance is the ongoing process of believing in the worth and value of Jesus, and then turning accordingly.

READ. THINK. DISCUSS.

What's the difference between walking away from something and turning toward something?

Why must true repentance be based in faith in order for it to stick?

What's the biggest obstacle you have in believing that Jesus is better than what you're turning away from?

What's God lovingly calling you to repent from?

How would you describe repentance to a non-Christian? What examples would you give to illustrate it?

2.4 SAVED

You can almost hear the voice of the revival preacher bouncing off the tent folds somewhere in the deep south as he describes the perils of hell and the fact that we're all headed there. Over and over again comes the question, "Have you been sa-a-a-a-aved-d-d-d-d-d!?!?!?!"

That word, maybe more than any other, has become part of the regular vernacular of Christian churches. We've used it so often that we don't even think about it anymore. We say "we got saved" at this particular moment or that particular event. We ask others if they've been saved to find out whether or not they're Christians. This particular word is so ingrained in the vocabulary of Christian subculture that it became the one word name of the 2004 satirical film mocking it.[16]

HELPLESS TO SAVE OURSELVES

Inside the church, we talk a lot about being saved, but outside the church, people are asking a very valid question: "Saved from what?" The word itself implies we need to avoid danger. Trouble. Hardship. That there is something we need to escape from. But you would have a hard time selling that to the vast majority of people outside the church, because their lives don't feel particularly perilous. They certainly don't see much of anything they need to escape from. Truth be told, the word that describes their lives best is something like "comfortable." So being "saved" doesn't resonate with them.

But just because we can't see the danger doesn't mean it's not there. In fact, isn't unforeseen danger really the worst kind? It's one matter to be walking through the African savanna and see a lion in the distance. A lion certainly isn't an animal you want to walk up on; so you stop, calm yourself, and slowly back away. You sense the danger of the situation, knowing you need to get out of it as quickly as possible.

But what if you aren't in the African savanna? What if you're in the South American rain forest, trudging your way through the thick underbrush? The roots, vines, and foliage are so thick that you never see the venomous snake coiled on the ground. Your boot comes down closer and closer and closer, and then . . .

You never saw it coming. Clearly, the unexpected is a worse sort of danger than the kind you're aware of. But there's another difference in these two dangerous situations. In the first, you can play a part in saving yourself from danger because you're aware of the situation. You can slowly back away. Or you can turn and run. But in the second scenario, the danger is invisible, meaning you need to be saved, or rescued from danger.

In Ephesians 2:1-3, Paul described all of humanity as being in peril and helpless to save itself:

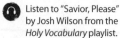

Listen to "Savior, Please" by Josh Wilson from the *Holy Vocabulary* playlist.

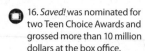

16. *Saved!* was nominated for two Teen Choice Awards and grossed more than 10 million dollars at the box office.

> "And you were dead in your trespasses and sins in which you previously walked according to this worldly age, according to the ruler of the atmospheric domain, the spirit now working in the disobedient. We too all previously lived among them in our fleshly desires, carrying out the inclinations of our flesh and thoughts, and by nature we were children under wrath, as the others were also."

Paul depicted a very dire situation. Notice the specific word the Bible used to describe the human condition: dead. If that word doesn't speak to the severity and desperation of our situation, then surely nothing does. In fact, this word moves our situation well past desperate and into the territory of hopeless. This description from Ephesians 2 serves to contradict a well-known cultural axiom: Christianity is a crutch for the weak.

When people make this statement, they usually intend it as an insult. They mean that people believe in God, and in particular Jesus, because they need something to believe in. In this mind-set, such people don't have the intestinal fortitude to accept the randomness of life, so they fabricate in their minds this idea of a sovereign and loving God who is in control of events. They lean on this belief like a crutch because they aren't strong enough to withstand the realities of our world.

But according to Ephesians 2, Christianity isn't a crutch for the weak, because that statement isn't insulting enough. A crutch gives us far too much credit and robs the gospel of its full implication and power. Christianity isn't a crutch for the weak; it's a stretcher for the dead. We are so spiritually dead that we aren't even aware that we need to be saved. We need God to step into that deadness to make us aware of the peril.

JESUS, OUR SAVIOR

We often think about being saved like this: We're floating in the sea of sin and death about to drown when, with our last bit of strength, we cry out to Jesus who throws us a life preserver. That's certainly a situation from which we would need to be saved, but that's not what we see in this passage of Scripture. Instead, the picture here is of a corpse, bloated and floating face down in the sea. No strength. No power. No hope. Then Jesus pulls that corpse out of the water, out of sin and death, and breathes new life into it. That's what it means to be saved.

And that's the promise of the gospel. Thankfully, Ephesians 2 doesn't stop in verse 3 with the description of our dead selves.[17] Paul continues:

> "But God, who is abundant in mercy, because of His great love that He had for us, made us alive with the Messiah even though we were dead in trespasses. By grace you are saved!" (Ephesians 2:4-5).

---

 17. The apostle Paul uses the word "saved" 21 times in his New Testament letters (*biblegateway.com*).

Paul transitions with two of the most amazing words in all of Scripture: "But God . . ." We were dead, but God . . . We had no hope, but God . . . We couldn't rescue ourselves, but God . . .

The gospel doesn't claim to help the weak; it claims to make the dead alive. Only when we begin to see ourselves in our true form—lifeless apart from God—do we begin to see Jesus not as the key to a better life. Not as a sage who teaches about love. Not as a miracle worker only concerned with the alleviation of human suffering. We see Jesus as our Savior.

Jesus jumped into that proverbial ocean where our corpse was floating. And when He did, He got really, really wet. He immersed Himself in that sea of sin and death. He went under the water and boosted us up to safety. And with His last breath, He breathed life into our spiritual bodies. Jesus took our place as the floating corpse. He didn't come out unscathed from the rescue; it cost Him His life. He floated in our place in sin and death.

Jesus jumped in and saved us from death. And that death is inherent in us because of our sin, which He also saves us from. Even if we wanted to stop sinning we couldn't, because it's in our nature—the deepest parts of who we are—to rebel against the loving rule of God. In that sense, Jesus saves us from ourselves, too. From our selfishness. From our continued insistence that we know how to run our lives. From our ego-centric approach to life and our correspondingly small vision of what life is really about. But there's something else we need to be saved from, a danger far less acknowledged, and much more uncomfortable, than these others. We need to be saved from the wrath of God.

The first passage of Ephesians 2 reminds us that we are "children under wrath." Whose wrath might that be? Whose anger? Whose unquenchable fire of just condemnation? It's God's. In His absolute righteousness, God will punish transgression and sin. And the wrath of God is something we frankly do not want to be under. The crushing weight of His judgment is staring us in the face, and rightly so, because we have offended Him with our extreme unfaithfulness. But here is the amazing thing: God has stooped low to meet us in our sin. God has delivered us—saved us—from His own wrath. And He has done so at extreme cost to Himself. He is not only just, but the One who justifies those who are justifiably condemned.[18] Amazing.

Jesus, the Great Rescuer, has come, and He saves us from spiritual death by giving us spiritual life forever with Him. Never stop telling people you're saved. Just start telling them what you're saved from and about the One who saved you.

 "I am the door. If anyone enters by Me, he will be saved and will come in and go out and find pasture" (John 10:9).

 18. Paul sums this up in Romans 3:23-26.

READ. THINK. DISCUSS.

What do you think most people's opinion is of the word "saved" when used in a religious context?

What is your "But God" moment?

What value is there in regularly thinking about what you have been saved from?

Why is understanding the concepts behind the word "saved" essential for understanding the gospel?

2.5 BELIEVE

Believe (verb): "to have confidence in the truth, the existence, or the reliability of something, although without absolute proof."[19] Believing is what we do when we put our faith or trust in something else. We believe countless things in our lives, beginning when we're young: "I believe in Santa"—and continuing well into our grown up lives—"I believe in our government's checks and balances system" or "I believe in love at first sight."

Belief is the crux of our life in Christ. We don't come into the family of God because of what we do or don't do, our economic status or lack thereof, or our nation of origin. Even our past has no bearing on our entrance into God's family. What does have bearing, however, is what we believe.

That was the essence of Paul's thesis statement for the Book of Romans:

> **"For I am not ashamed of the gospel, because it is God's power for salvation to everyone *who believes*, first to the Jew, and also to the Greek. For in it God's righteousness is revealed from faith to faith, just as it is written: The righteous will live by faith" (Romans 1:16-17, emphasis added).**

We believe, and therefore we are saved. That's the crucial role of belief in our spiritual lives.

IT'S ALL SPIRITUAL

Before we get into the specifics of what we believe, let's first define what is meant by the phrase "spiritual lives."

Spiritual is a popular word. Paul used it repeatedly throughout Romans. But I'm pretty sure he used it in a different way than how it's being thrown around today. When Paul used the word, he did so in conjunction with the gospel of Jesus Christ and in that context alone, so there was an inherent exclusivity to his terminology. But *spiritual* can mean almost anything these days. One can be spiritual without any commitment and belief in absolute truth.

Spiritual people can be subscribers to any number of world religions.[20] Being spiritual doesn't require a person to believe anything in particular, but just to believe in general. In that scenario, *believing* is the end in itself. There is value in believing, regardless of what you believe in. Consequently, there are a lot of very spiritual people walking around whose "faith" is really only marked by occasional pensive looks into the sky and the propensity to read a philosophy book once in a while. It's not enough to "just believe." It's important to believe in something. And if you believe that there is such a thing as good and evil, right and wrong, it's important to believe in the "right" something.

---

19. From *dictionary.com*.

 20. *Adherents.com* lists 22 major world religions with at least 500 thousand adherents each.

In Romans 1:16-17, Paul defined that right something as the gospel—that Jesus Christ, the Son of God, came to earth and lived a perfect life and died a sinner's death. In so doing, He took on Himself the just punishment for our sins. It is by believing in Him that we are forgiven as He takes our sin upon Himself and grants us His righteousness. This is the belief our salvation is contingent on.[21]

Unfortunately most of us stop there. We believe those facts above, and because we do, we've got a one-way ticket to heaven (or more importantly, a ticket out of hell). But notice what else Paul says in that passage about believing. Not only is believing the way to salvation, but it is the way of life for Christians, for "the righteous will live by faith." *Faith* is another way of saying *belief*.

Most of us live our lives in a sort of hybrid version of true Christianity—something like Christian legalism. You may be thinking that those two terms contradict each other, and you're right. They do. Christianity, as we've already said, isn't about what you do, it's about what you believe. And legalism by its very definition is contrary to that, because a legalist is one who seeks to earn the favor of God through personal merits. So how do those things fit together?

Actually, they fit together quite nicely. Just look at most of our lives. We would agree that we've been saved by grace through faith and that's why we're going to heaven. Not because of anything we've done. But that's where believing usually ends for us. From that point on, we live our lives like God's favor is now dependent, after that initial display of belief, on our works. So we work hard at being good Christians so that God will like us. See? Christian legalism.

Part of the reason we try so hard to be good Christians is because it's a lot easier to work than it is to live by belief alone. When you work, you have something quantifiable. Something measurable. Something to hold up at the end of the day to validate the way you spent your time. We think we could make God like us more by doing good stuff. But when you believe? Well, belief by its very nature operates in the realm of the unseen.[22] And that's just not concrete enough for us.

So we should believe. But that's easier said than done. Exactly how do we believe? And how do we believe in such a way that our whole lives—not just our salvation—is based on faith?

THE ACT OF BELIEF

This is where it gets a little problematic, because we love to talk about *what* to believe. We have oodles of classes, schools, studies, and bookstores filled with what to believe. But if believing isn't just about salvation but an entire way of life, it seems to me that we should not only ask what to believe, but *how* to believe. So once again—if believing is so important, how do you do it? And how do you do it on a moment by moment basis?

 21. The Nicene Creed, drafted in A.D. 325 and modified in A.D. 381, sums up the core beliefs of Christianity. Read it at *creeds.net*.

 22. A 2006 Baylor University survey found that 62.9 percent of non-religious Americans believe in God or a higher power.

It's a tricky question, right? Believing isn't like cooking or riding a bike or playing left field where there's a step-by-step process to follow. The Greeks thought believing involved the intellect. We've adopted the same idea into our English understanding, that belief is about assenting to a certain set of facts which you hold to be true. So the "how" of believing, from that mind-set, involves proof.

But the Hebrew mind-set is different. Take a look at two ways the root word for "believe" is used in the Old Testament:

> **"Abram believed the LORD, and He credited it to him as righteousness"** (Genesis 15:6).

> **"When Moses' hands grew heavy, they took a stone and put it under him, and he sat down on it. Then Aaron and Hur supported his hands, one on one side and one on the other so that his hands remained steady until the sun went down"** (Exodus 17:12).

The first usage is fairly straightforward. The second one? Not as obvious. In the Exodus 17 passage, the Israelites were at war against the Amalekites. As long as Moses' arm was raised, the Israelites were winning the battle, but when he lowered his arm, the Amalekites strengthened. The Israelites' victory depended on the steadiness of Moses' arm. The Hebrew word translated "remained steady" in Exodus 17:12 is the same word translated "believed" in Genesis 15:6. Now that's interesting, and quite revelatory about the Hebrew concept of belief. To the Hebrews, belief wasn't something one floated in and out of. It also wasn't strictly intellectual. Belief was challenging and required perseverance. Belief was about remaining steady.

So what is the answer to the initial question of how we believe? We work at it. And sometimes—many times—that work is hard. It's as hard as holding your hands above your head for an entire day. It's hard to believe God when the circumstances of life are as heavy as your arms at 3 p.m.

THE POWER TO BELIEVE

For the Christian, belief is a choice. And you have the power to exercise that choice in every arena of life. When tempted to be greedy with your finances, you have to make a choice to believe that it's better to give than receive. When tempted to think that your marriage has grown stale and that you would be more fulfilled outside of it, you have to make a choice to believe that God put you in relationship with your spouse. When tempted to overeat and indulge yourself, you have to make a choice to believe that your body is a temple of the Holy Spirit and should be treated as such. And the list goes on and on.

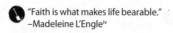
"Faith is what makes life bearable."
–Madeleine L'Engle[iv]

Listen to "I Believe" by Jonny Lang
from the *Holy Vocabulary* playlist.

The temptation is for us to try and supplant belief with our works. But God's intent is for belief to be at the center of everything we do, even those things that seem like works. Make no mistake—the Christian life is work. But many of us are working hard at the wrong thing. We're working hard not to sin. We're working hard to be generous. We're working hard to read the Bible.

We should be working hard to believe in each and every one of those situations. We must believe that in each of those individual moments, God's resources of grace, power, patience, hope, and endurance won't run dry. We believe in Him as the Great Supplier of what we need, and we do so one need at a time. In this we see the true centrality of Jesus in salvation, for He is the Initiator, the Sustainer, and the Goal of our belief.

Like Moses, we aren't left to fend for ourselves as we struggle to believe. Belief, just like the rest of salvation, is a gift of God that comes to us by His grace and grace alone. After that point we are armed with the power of the Holy Spirit. The same power that raised Christ from the dead empowers us to believe.

READ. THINK. DISCUSS.

If someone were to ask you how important is belief to Christianity, what would you say?

How about if they asked you what you believe? How would you respond?

What does it mean to "live by faith"?

Can you think of a time when you had to work hard to believe? What were the circumstances?

Think about your everyday life. How would your perspective change if you tried to integrate faith into everything you did?

SESSION THREE HOLY VOCABULARY

WHO IS THIS JESUS?

Messiah. Son of God. Son of man. Prince of peace. Immanuel. Lion of Judah. Savior. Wonderful Counselor. Lamb of God. The Word. Light of the world. King of kings. Good Shepherd. Christ. Yeshua. Lord of lords. Rabbi. Teacher. Alpha. Omega.

Talk about some nicknames. These barely scratch the surface of what Jesus is called in Scripture. Each one gives us a small clue as to His identity, an identity so complex that it's no wonder we're left questioning, "Who is this man?"

It's a fundamental question to answer, one people have wrestled with for thousands of years. When Jesus burst onto the scene, people had questions. There He was miracling a meal out of a few meager loaves and fish in order to feed thousands. Calming the wind and waves. Healing the sick. Raising the dead. And teaching in a fearless, authoritative manner that the people had never seen before.

Some in Jesus' time argued He was a political leader who came to deliver the nation of Israel from Roman rule. Others saw Him as the reincarnation of one of the great prophets of old. Still others considered Him to be demon-possessed, a messenger of Satan sent to lead people down the road of blasphemy. To me, it seems like not much has changed.

The name "Jesus" is arguably the most controversial, polarizing name out there. Most people don't have a problem talking about God. They have their own ideas about who He is. Bring Jesus' name up, though, and you're likely to enter the realm of controversy.

People have a tendency to make Jesus fit their desires and agendas—be it anything from passivism to social justice. And the history books certainly affirm that a great teacher walked the dusty roads of Palestine. But when you look for Jesus in Scripture, be prepared to find someone who really isn't interested in fitting into agendas or human-created boxes. You find a Jesus who wasn't just a teacher, prophet, good man, or peacekeeper, but someone who called Himself "the Son of God" (John 10:36).

Life and death literally hang in the balance as we try to understand the identity of this carpenter-teacher from Nazareth and how His life changed the eternal outcome of ours. The words in this session are big, "churchy" words. But their meanings hold the key to our salvation.

3.1 BEGOTTEN

"For God loved the world in this way: He gave His One and Only Son … "

So goes John 3:16, the most familiar verse in the Bible. If you look at more recent translations, you see that the phrase "One and Only" replaced the word "begotten" (KJV). But perhaps "begotten" holds a special place in your vocabulary from when you memorized John 3:16 back in the day, while earning stars and check marks on the felt board of your Sunday School room.

Begotten. Now there's a word that sounds "churchy" if ever there was one. It harkens back to the genealogies of the Old Testament where so-and-so begat so-and-so junior.[1] John, the Gospel writer, evidently thought it was an important word. In this pivotal verse, when he described who God appointed to carry out His salvation of the world, John didn't just say "His Son." He emphasized that Jesus is God's "only *begotten* Son." Apparently Jesus' "begotten-ness" is worth noting. However, the definition of begotten doesn't give us much to work with.

Begotten means bred. Spawned. Reproduced. My begotten sons are Joshua and Christian, and their "begotten-ness" comes from the fact that they are my boys. It's a pretty boring definition when you think about it. So why did John choose this adjective? Why not something more flashy?

Because "begetting" speaks to something's original nature. As C. S. Lewis pointed out, "When you beget, you beget something of the same kind as yourself. A man begets human babies, a beaver begets little beavers and a bird begets eggs which turn into little birds."[2] We reproduce our own kind, our own nature. Nobody goes to the delivery room of a hospital expecting to bring a dolphin home with them.

In the Person of Jesus, God begat God, meaning Jesus is fully divine. This is fundamental to understanding the identity of Jesus, an identity which has been under attack from the very beginning.

THE SON OF GOD

Many have tried to make Jesus out to be simply a great teacher. Or a prophet. Or a sage. But the biblical truth is inescapable: As the only begotten Son of God, Jesus Christ is divine in nature. And He's unique in that aspect.

As Christians, we are the children of God, but we were adopted into the family. Not Jesus. As the begotten One, He shares God's nature. He is one-third of the Trinity, meaning Jesus is God. Paul hammered this point home in the Book of Colossians, a letter written to a city

---

1. See Genesis chapters 4, 5, and 10 for examples. Other translations read "fathered" or "was the father to."

2. C. S. Lewis, *Mere Christianity* (Broadman & Holman Publishers, 1996), 138.

with all kinds of competing philosophies. Teachers in Colossae argued that angels should be worshiped; magic holidays had to be celebrated, and grotesque rituals had to be performed to get into God's inner circle; and only a select few possessed special spiritual knowledge.

Into this fray of ideologies Paul wrote over and over the name that trumps every other name in the universe: Jesus. Jesus. Jesus. That's what Colossians is really about. It's about how Jesus is the center, or the linchpin of reality as we know it. Take out Jesus and the very fabric of everything we know to be true about Christianity would fall apart, for "by Him all things hold together" (Colossians 1:17).

Jesus is worthy of supremacy in all things, says Paul, because "He is the image of the invisible God" (Colossians 1:15). God "was pleased to have all His fullness dwell in [His Son]" (Colossians 1:19). And in Jesus, "all the fullness of the Deity lives in bodily form" (Colossians 2:9, NIV). Not once, not twice, but three times in these two chapters Paul emphasizes the identity of Jesus as God.

Let's say it again: Jesus Christ is God. This revelation isn't something we read only in the writings of Paul.

IN THE BEGINNING

The apostle John says the same thing in his Gospel. In fact, the Gospel of John was written to combat a heretical teaching that Jesus was a great man but not God. Well, John made his feelings about that belief clear from the first sentence of his book:

> "In the beginning was the Word, and the Word was with God, and the Word was God" (John 1:1).

And then later in the same chapter,

> "The Word became flesh and took up residence among us" (John 1:14).

Those words came before he wrote about Jesus being "begotten."

These verses also point out that Jesus' "begotten-ness" isn't about His being born at a certain time in history. There has never been a time when Jesus did not exist. He is eternal in the same way that the Father and Spirit are eternal. He is at once God and with God from before the beginning of forever. But why call Jesus "the Word"? What does that have to do with the subject of His identity? Everything.

Think about it this way: In every relationship, you have a certain amount of control over what people know about you. You can tell them as much or as little as you like, which lets

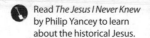

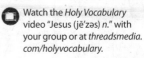

Read *The Jesus I Never Knew* by Philip Yancey to learn about the historical Jesus.

Watch the *Holy Vocabulary* video "Jesus (jē'zəs) n." with your group or at *threadsmedia. com/holyvocabulary*.

them know you as fully or as vaguely as you want. Your choice of words dictates whether you'll live in surface level, superficial relationships, or in deep and authentic ones. Your words are the doorway to intimacy with others.

John had a couple of reasons for describing Jesus as "the Word." Because the primary audience of the Gospel was Greek, he used a word that had great meaning for them. To the Greek mind-set, the *logos*, or word, was very significant, for the *logos* was the source of philosophical ideas and intelligence, both of which held paramount importance in Greek culture. And Jesus sits at the center of such things.

When we think of words, though, we think of the devices we use to express things. This book is a study of the words we use to talk about Christianity. By calling Jesus "the Word," John was also referring to Him as the expression of God to the world. When Jesus came and dwelt among us, it was God's way of expressing part of Himself to the world.[3]

In presenting Jesus as the Word who was both with God and at the same time was God, John was saying simply this: If you want to know who God is, or if you want to walk in intimacy with Him, just look at Jesus. He's the revelation of God.

ONE WITH GOD

Jesus knew He was God incarnate, too. He proclaimed it, but not everyone around Him was happy about such claims. John 8 is another passage that tells about the identity of Jesus. People gathered around Him and charged that His extraordinary ability to work miracles came from demons. Jesus made a radical statement in verse 51, saying:

> **"I assure you: If anyone keeps My word, he will never see death—ever!"**

The Jews were shocked. They retorted that Jesus was arrogant. After all, they reasoned, Abraham was the greatest person they could think of and he died. But Jesus responded by saying that even Abraham rejoiced in the day of Jesus' coming.

That idea was laughable to Jesus' audience. Abraham had been dead for centuries, yet Jesus, who was only around 30 years old, claimed to have seen him. Who did Jesus think He was? His response incensed the crowd:

> **"I assure you: Before Abraham was, I am"** (John 8:58).

That claim made the people so mad that they tried to kill Jesus. Why? Even though Jesus' statement is a little confusing, it doesn't seem like one that warrants death. But when Jesus said those two words, "I am," He invoked the precious name of God Almighty, the name

---

 3. In John 1:1-5, John describes Jesus' coming with words that harken back to creation, like "life," "light," and "darkness."

that no Jewish person dared to utter, and applied it to Himself. It was the same name that God told Moses to call Him in Exodus 3. It was the same name that had defined the God of the Jews for centuries. Jesus very clearly said: "I, Jesus, am the same as your God. I am 'I Am.'"

As the begotten Son of God, Jesus Christ is unique in the universe. He's divine. He's I Am. And when we look at Jesus, we see God's final and complete revelation of Himself.

READ. THINK. DISCUSS.

Why do you think the idea that Jesus is God is so unpopular in modern culture?

How does life change once you fully accept that Jesus Christ is God?

What implications does the deity of Jesus have for the way we worship God?

What is the biggest spiritual truth you glean from John's description of Jesus as "the Word"?

3.2 CROSS

The cross is the universal symbol of Christianity. Whether you're in Kenya, Spain, India, or Memphis, Tennessee, when you see a cross you know a church is nearby. Such familiarity also means big bucks. Cross accessories are everywhere. Earrings, necklaces, rings, and T-shirts all bear the emblem. You can find the cross on bumper stickers, in logos of Christian companies, and intertwined in people's tribal tattoos.

It's pretty ironic how "cross-crazy" we seem, considering how someone in the first century would have viewed those two wooden beams nailed together. Far from a piece of art or an accessory to an outfit, the cross in its original form was a mark of disgrace, pain, and violence. It was the primary method of public execution in Jesus' day, and a very inhumane method at that. Crucifixion is the most brutal form of punishment ever devised, designed to inflict the maximum amount of pain and suffering on the unfortunate person hanging on it.

Our fondness of the cross would be shocking to anyone from that time period. It would be tastelessly equivalent to someone in our culture wearing an electric chair on a chain around her neck or tattooing his bicep with a hangman's noose. We have lost the shocking nature of the cross and have tamed it down to something more palpable.

A CURSED DEATH

But it's not palpable. The cross is about blood, guts, tears, and suffering. It's fundamentally about death, but not just any death. The cross is about a cursed death. That's what Paul wrote in Galatians 3:13:

> **"Christ has redeemed us from the curse of the law by becoming a curse for us, because it is written: 'Cursed is everyone who is hung on a tree.'"**

Paul quoted Deuteronomy 21:23, which very explicitly says that whoever hangs on the cross "is under God's curse." That's harsh language to describe the death of the only One who has ever lived perfectly on this earth.[4] People might quickly describe Jesus' death as unfortunate or unfair. From the Christian perspective, we might describe it as glorious, loving, or redemptive. But neither group—Christians or non-Christians—is likely to describe the crucifixion as a curse from God.

How could God curse His own Son? The words leave a bad taste in our mouths. But Jesus acknowledged God's curse while He was hanging on the cross that day:

> **"And at three Jesus cried out with a loud voice, 'Eloi, Eloi, lemá sabachtháni?' which is translated, 'My God, My God, why have You forsaken Me?'"** (Mark 15:34).

....

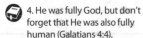 4. He was fully God, but don't forget that He was also fully human (Galatians 4:4).

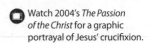 Watch 2004's *The Passion of the Christ* for a graphic portrayal of Jesus' crucifixion.

None of us will ever experience such a cry of anguish. We might walk through physical, emotional, and spiritual pain, but nothing will rival this moment for the Messiah. Jesus wasn't just crying out about His physical torment. In His words we find the true extent of His pain—He was forsaken by His Father.

In some mysterious way that I don't fully understand, there was a break in the Trinity at the cross. The Son, who had existed from all eternity in perfect love and fellowship with the Father and Spirit, was crushed under the weight of sin. For in those hours at Calvary,[5] God poured out a millennia of stored up and justified wrath and punishment for sin onto His beloved Son.[6]

Jesus became a curse at the cross. That statement contains another important word for us to look at. Jesus *became* a curse; He wasn't just cursed. Let me explain the difference between those two statements.

My older son loves to put on his Jedi costume. He brandishes his light saber and wields it at imaginary foes (who often unfortunately take the form of his younger sister). He fights and he imagines, but he doesn't *become* an actual Jedi. He acts like one. He thinks of himself as one. But to become one? Well, *becoming* is a different matter. It requires a change in the fundamental reality and identity of someone.

Jesus actually *became* a curse on the cross. He took on all the world's hate, anger, malice, murder, lust, laziness, and every other sin imaginable. The clean became dirty. The pure became tainted. And the physical pain of the cross was nothing compared to the breaking of fellowship with the Father that came as a result. That's what we hang around our necks and put on our cars. That's what we accessorize with.

THE CROSS SETS US FREE

Before you get out the razor blade for your bumper and make an appointment at the tattoo removal center, let's examine the other side of the cross. For just as Jesus *became* a curse that day at Calvary, we become His righteousness:

"He made the One who did not know sin to be sin for us, so that we might become the righteousness of God in Him" (2 Corinthians 5:21).

It's amazing to think that the cross is also about us becoming righteous. I think sometimes we look at the cross and think of it exclusively in terms of forgiveness. We should do that, because that's where our forgiveness for sin has its basis. Without the cross, we would still be cursed for our sinful nature and the sinful acts that come from it. But the cross takes us beyond forgiveness. We aren't just forgiven. We're righteous, free from the sinful nature that once bound us and the guilt that accompanied it. Because of Jesus' work on the

---

 5. Read the account of the crucifixion in Matthew 27:33-50 or John 19:17-30.

 6. "For Christ also suffered for sins once for all, the righteous for the unrighteous, that He might bring you to God" (1 Peter 3:18).

 "All God's plans have the mark of the cross on them, and all His plans have death to self in them." –E. M. Bounds[v]

cross, when God looks at us He sees the righteousness of Christ. The cross is the place where sin is exchanged for righteousness.

How strange that such a cosmic, eternal, heart-changing act would happen on a structure that was intended to inflict the worst pain imaginable. What a huge reversal of fortune, that the very object used for punishment became the salvation of the world in Christ. Strange, weird, illogical, yes—but that's exactly what God intended.

THERE IS POWER IN THE BLOOD
Paul had something else to say about the cross:

> "For to those who are perishing the message of the cross is foolishness, but to us who are being saved it is God's power. For it is written: 'I will destroy the wisdom of the wise, and I will set aside the understanding of the experts. Where is the philosopher? Where is the scholar? Where is the debater of this age?" (1 Corinthians 1:18-20).

The unfathomable mystery of the cross isn't that Jesus, the Son of God, was killed on it, but that three days later He came back to life. In the resurrection, Jesus conquered death once and for all, making His sacrifice on our behalf permanent:

> "For Christ's love compels us, since we have reached this conclusion: if One died for all, then all died. And He died for all so that those who live should no longer live for themselves, but for the One who died for them and was raised" (2 Corinthians 5:14-15).

Because of His power over death, we will get to experience eternal life.[7] This is the message of the cross that Paul knows sounds like foolishness to some, but brings the powerful saving grace of God to those who believe. God chose the most unlikely of instruments to accomplish the most unlikely of actions. In doing so, He made sure that He, and only He, would receive the glory for it. No one else could do this. No one else would dare. But God? God used the cross to prove Himself wise, good, and just beyond all reckoning.

The cross is an inseparable part of the gospel. It's the place where the final and ultimate statement about the love and justice of God was made. It's the place where our redemption and salvation was bought. And the event that took place on it is the climax of the Christian message. As Paul said:

> "For I determined to know nothing among you except Jesus Christ and Him crucified" (1 Corinthians 2:2).

 Listen to "Lead Me to the Cross" by Cori Moon from the *Holy Vocabulary* playlist.

 7. Check out Philippians 3 for a powerful word from Paul about the importance of knowing the resurrected Christ.

READ. THINK. DISCUSS.

Why is the crucifixion the sum total of the Christian message?

How, as Christians, should we view the cross?

What implications does the cross have for the way you live day in and day out?

What are some ways you can remind yourself of the cross more often?

3.3 GRACE

"Grace and peace." That two-word salutation is how the apostle Paul began much of his correspondence recorded in the New Testament. "Grace and peace" was Paul's greeting to his audience, in the same way that we might write, "Dear . . . ," or "To Whom It May Concern." Why is that? Were they just convenient and poetic words, a way to say "Hey there!" with a little more class? Or is there something more?

I would suggest that these two words—grace and peace—are a summation of the gospel. If that's true, then with the opening of each letter Paul conjures up a vivid reminder for his audience of what they all (as hopelessly lost sinners and subsequently found children of God) have in common. Grace and peace.[8]

GOD'S FREE GIFT TO US

The Greek word for grace is *charis*, and there's no question of its importance in biblical theology. *Charis* appears 116 times in the New Testament. There's a lot about grace in Scripture because it's the message of Jesus.

Grace means favor. It means acceptance. It means giving. Grace is free in the sense that something done or given in grace is done so without expecting to receive anything in return. Grace isn't dependent on the way it's received, the moral goodness of the one receiving it, or even that person's ability to rightly say, "Thank you." The only thing grace is dependent on is the generosity of the giver.

Good thing for us that God is an endless well of generosity. Because of grace, the sun came up this morning. The same is true for your beating heart, rain, the changing of the seasons, and the earth's steady rotation. These are what we call God's "common graces," and they aren't motivated by any good thing humanity's done. But for the Christ-follower, grace goes beyond the common and enters into the scandalous.

J. I. Packer wrote, "God is good to all in some ways and to some in all ways."[9] The common graces are the "some ways" He's good to everyone, but for the people who believe in Him, He's good in "all ways." Every other religion in the world boils down to a sort of cosmic barter system. People bring their good stuff to their god, whether it's good actions, good money, or good sacrifices, and in exchange their god gives them some of its good stuff.

Not so in Christianity. As a grace-based belief system, Christianity is built solely on the extravagant goodness of God. Nothing in us motivates God's grace, and nothing we do can pay Him back. The only part we play in grace is receiving it:

 8. *Peace* follows *grace* in Paul's greetings, because it's only possible through God's grace.

9. J. I. Packer, *Knowing God* (Downers Grove, Ill: InterVarsity Press, 1973), 162.

> "For by grace you are saved through faith, and this is not from yourselves; it is God's gift—not from works, so that no one can boast" (Ephesians 2:8-9).

Jesus lived out this truth in His ministry. When He healed the sick, He didn't do so on the basis of their righteousness. When He fed the hungry, He didn't do so with the intent to have them repay Him. And when He offers salvation to the world, He doesn't make a qualification about who can receive it. Salvation is framed in terms of "whosoever." Jesus invites the "weary and burdened" to lay their yokes on Him (Matthew 11:28). His life, ministry, death, and resurrection display the grace of God to a hopelessly lost world.

THE STRUGGLE TO ACCEPT

What a tremendous reality! The free gift of God given to us—unmerited favor through Jesus Christ. Why is it, then, that so many of us choose to live in the opposite manner of grace?

The opposite of grace is legalism—the belief that our works will earn us God's favor. His love. His blessing. If we're honest, living legalistically is often more comfortable for us than living in grace. We like having a measuring stick for how good we're doing at being Christians. We like to check things off our lists to prove we're making progress. This legalistic way of thinking is so easy, argues pastor and author Chuck Swindoll in his book *The Grace Awakening*, because of the pride ingrained within us:

> "Grace says you have nothing to give, nothing to earn, nothing to pay. You couldn't if you tried! . . . Salvation is a free gift. You simply lay hold of what Christ has provided. Period. And yet the heretical doctrine of works goes on all around the world and always will. It is effective because the pride of men and women is so strong. We simply *have* to *do* something in order to feel right about it. It just doesn't make good humanistic sense to get something valuable for nothing."[10]

Everything in our nature fights the great promise of grace. But when we learn to live by grace alone, we are able to wholeheartedly believe in God's saving grace rather than try to earn it. We're enabled to trust His promises rather than accumulate "good Christian" points. And we're forced to be humble in who we are as His children rather than take pride in what good Christians we are.

IN NEED OF GRACE

In addition to our legalistic bent, truly accepting grace is difficult for us because deep in our hearts, we really don't think we're that bad. We're not thieves. We're not murderers. We're just regular people who occasionally do the wrong thing. We're pretty good, so what need do we really have for grace? But let's examine that thought process more closely.

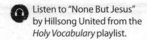 Listen to "None But Jesus" by Hillsong United from the *Holy Vocabulary* playlist.

10. Charles R. Swindoll, *The Grace Awakening* (Nashville: W Publishing Group, 2003), 79-80.

What does it really mean to be a "pretty good person"? Does it mean you help others? Does it mean you give away some money? Does it mean you are faithful to your spouse? It's tough to pin down, but when we consider ourselves to be "pretty good," we generally do so in comparison to others. Our mind-set tends to be something like, *Well, at least I'm not like that person. I'm not as bad as she is.*

The problem is, we aren't measured against other people. How everyone else is doing is insignificant, for the ruler of righteousness isn't laid up against them. It's laid against the perfect standard of God Almighty. And regardless of how everyone else is doing, we fall pretty short when compared to God.

Furthermore, though we may not be doing actions we deem as bad as others', the motivation behind what we do is key. Are our intentions in good behavior pure, or do we want others to see how good we are? Are our motives for obeying God unblemished, or are we trying to rack up grace points? If we were honest and looked at all the things that make us "not that bad," we'd find that even when we're doing the right thing, we're often doing it for the wrong reason. In the words of the prophet Isaiah:

> **"All of us have become like something unclean, and all our righteous acts are like a polluted garment; all of us wither like a leaf, and our iniquities carry us away like the wind" (Isaiah 64:6).**[11]

FREEDOM TO LIVE OBEDIENTLY

Paul understood our need for God's grace and the struggle to accept it, and those truths were at the core of his message. But they got him into trouble on many occasions. He consistently preached about grace alone through faith alone in Christ alone, and people stood in opposition.

Paul was accused of preaching a doctrinal system called *antinomianism*, the belief that people were under no obligation to obey any moral or ethical rules of conduct. That charge was aimed at Paul's preaching because, as his opponents reasoned, talking so much about grace would lead people to believe that they could do whatever they wanted with no repercussions.

In a way, I suppose they were right. If we live under grace, we can do whatever we want and expect God to forgive us. Some people refer to this mind-set as "grace abuse." The problem with this line of thinking lies in the definition of "whatever we want to do." See, the grace of God is a transformative grace. God's grace takes our sinful desires and, through time, makes them into desires of goodness and love. By His grace, we are transformed into people who actually *want* to do the right thing instead of people who *have* to do the right thing.

---

 11. Literally, Isaiah claimed our righteous acts are like a used menstrual rag. That sure puts our arrogance in its place.

Because of grace, we no longer work to earn divine approval. We know we already have it. We act because God's grace has changed us. As Titus 2:11-13 says:

> "For the grace of God has appeared, with salvation for all people, instructing us to deny godlessness and worldly lusts and to live in a sensible, righteous, and godly way in the present age, while we wait for the blessed hope and the appearing of the glory of our great God and Savior, Jesus Christ."

Grace doesn't license us for immorality; it teaches us godliness. That's a lesson we'll spend our whole lives learning, which is why we need God's grace, every day. We need it like the dry ground needs water from heaven. Praise be to God that, in Jesus, He opened up His grace reservoir for His kids. Because He did, we don't have to walk in condemnation. The gospel brings us confidence, not because we're good people, but because Jesus was good on our behalf.

READ. THINK. DISCUSS.

Do you tend to lean more toward the abuse of grace or the inability to accept grace? Why?

Why do you think people find it so difficult to live by grace?

How would our relationships with others be affected if we truly understood grace?

What does someone's relationship with Jesus look like when they truly accept grace?

What's the relationship between grace and faith?

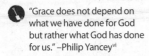

"Grace does not depend on what we have done for God but rather what God has done for us." –Philip Yancey[vi]

3.4 PROPITIATION

Propitiation may be the most important word to understand if you want to get to the heart of the gospel of Jesus Christ. But let's be honest—most of us have no idea what that word means, even if we've used it in an impressive gospel presentation or two. You likely get that blank, distant look on your face when your preacher describes how Jesus was "the propitiation for your sins." I imagine it's the same look I get when the guy from the Geek Squad® tells me that my virtual disk is fragmented. What?

Part of the reason we have a hard time defining this term is because the actual word *propitiation* has been written out of many modern translations of Scripture by different phrases that soften its meaning. Take Romans 3:25, for example.[12] That verse is about Jesus' involvement in the satisfaction of God's wrath. But in a lot of translations, you don't find the word "propitiation." You find "sacrifice of atonement." Or "the mercy seat."

Those descriptions are fine, but they don't communicate quite as much as "propitiation." But even if the word itself doesn't appear in the translation of the Bible you carry, the concept is found throughout both the Old and New Testaments.

To get a handle on propitiation, let's start in an unlikely place: *King Kong*. The iconic 1933 film contains not only the greatest recorded scream on film by star Fay Wray, but also a great representation of propitiation. In the movie, a group of filmmakers set sail to find Skull Island, the setting for their film. With them is the beautiful young actress Ann Darrow. Upon finding the island, Ann is taken captive by the natives and tied to some columns, left as a sacrifice to the islanders' god. Then there's the classic scene when the god, aka giant gorilla, emerges, and Darrow screams like there's no tomorrow.[13] That story exemplifies propitiation.

THE SATISFACTION OF GOD'S WRATH

In a very basic sense, *propitiation* is the averting of wrath by sacrifice. The definition conjures up images of virgins tied up and left to die, raised knives and spilled blood, and angry gods who must be pacified. If that's what we think of as propitiation, you might be wondering where we find that in Christianity. The answer is both nowhere and all over the place.

First, the "nowhere." In some religious contexts, most notably those of Greek mythology, gods are selfish and vengeful beings. Humans live in a constant state of fear and apprehension, always trying to make sure they haven't offended the divine. And if they do, they rush to make amends for their sins so that nothing bad happens. Our God is not like that.

---

 12. Hebrews 2:17 is another example worth comparing.

13. Disney classics more your thing? King Triton offers himself as the propitiation for Ursula's wrath in *The Little Mermaid*.

When God proclaimed His character to Moses, this is what He said:

"Yahweh—Yahweh is a compassionate and gracious God, slow to anger and rich in faithful love and truth, maintaining faithful love to a thousand generations, forgiving wrongdoing, rebellion, and sin" (Exodus 34:6-7).

This is hardly the picture of the Greek pantheon of gods who were so quick to get bent out of shape, looking for any reason imaginable to strike humanity with thunderbolts. Nevertheless, God's description of Himself continued in verse 7:

"But He will not leave the guilty unpunished, bringing the consequences of the fathers' wrongdoing on the children and grandchildren to the third and fourth generation."

Though God isn't like the pagan gods, His wrath and judgment are very, very real. Unlike other religions, when the God of Israel gets angry, His anger is based on offenses of real righteousness and goodness. The anger and wrath of God are absolutely and completely justified and create the need for propitiation.[14]

OLD TESTAMENT PROPITIATION

The Day of Atonement described in the Old Testament was fundamentally about propitiation. The specifics of the yearly ceremony are recorded in Leviticus 16. In that passage, we see the solemn moment as Aaron, the high priest, stepped before the tent of the presence of the Lord with two goats chosen from the Israelite community. Aaron knew that if he hadn't followed the prescribed procedure correctly, he would die for his sin before God. I imagine his hands were a little shaky.

One of the goats was to be slaughtered. Aaron needed the goat's blood, because without blood there is no remission of sin (Hebrews 9:22). However, the second goat wouldn't be killed. Aaron would place his hands on its head and confess all of the people's sins, symbolically transferring the sins from the people onto the goat. Then the goat would be sent away, removing the sins from the people and sending it into the oblivion of the Sinai desert.

Really? That's how sin was gotten rid of? Call me Debbie Downer, but it seems like sin is a bigger deal than that. Think about how much lying, corruption, sexual indiscretion, and downright nastiness a nation of people can rack up over the course of an entire year. And all of that somehow magically disappeared with the death of one goat and the exile of another? That doesn't seem satisfactory to me. And it wasn't. Not to God, anyway. Centuries later, that's precisely what the writer of Hebrews wrote:

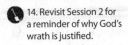 14. Revisit Session 2 for a reminder of why God's wrath is justified.

"It is impossible for the blood of bulls and goats to take away sins" (Hebrews 10:4).

So why the exercise? Why the slaughter? Why the poor goat voted off the island? The sacrificial system of the Old Testament illuminated our need for a more perfect and more complete propitiation for our sins and God's judgment.[15] For real propitiation to occur, a truly worthy substitute would have to bear the brunt of God's righteous wrath against His people. In so doing, fellowship with God would be restored.[16] This principle is the motivation for the life and death of Jesus Christ.

JESUS, OUR SUBSTITUTE

If you map out Jesus' travels, they might look a little random and haphazard. But make no mistake—the trajectory of His life constantly pointed toward Jerusalem and the cross. Luke reiterates this poignantly:

> **"As the time approached for him to be taken up to heaven, Jesus resolutely set out for Jerusalem" (Luke 9:51, NIV).**

I don't know how you imagine that scene, but I see Jesus turning His eyes toward the hills leading up to the holy city. I see Him pausing and putting His hand to His brow to shield His eyes from the sun. Then I imagine Him breathing deeply, exhaling slowly, and putting one foot in front of the other with a determined stride. Jesus knew the time had come for Him to fulfill His destiny. This was why He came to earth—to satisfy the wrath and justice of God.

The greatest difference between biblical propitiation and what we find in other major religions of the past and present is this: God not only received the propitiation His justice demands, but He planned it, carried it out, and took the punishment upon Himself.

We don't have to work to appease God or get Him to turn His wrath away from us. Rather, He chose to appease Himself by providing the means by which He might both fully love and save His children and at the same time not compromise the smallest bit of His just character. The crucifixion was the plan of the Father, Son, and Holy Spirit from the beginning of time. That's why Jesus can be called the Lamb slain from the creation of the world (Revelation 13:8). It's also why He wasn't shocked when the soldiers came for Him, and why He was so willing to give Himself up freely and completely (Matthew 26:52-56).

Jesus wasn't murdered by the Jews or the Romans. Sure, they held the nails and the spear, but killing Jesus wasn't their idea. God Himself planned the murder of His Son (Acts 2:23), and in so doing became not only our Creator but our Redeemer. Not only the One who was angry, but the propitiation that brought us peace. Propitiation is at the heart of the gospel and the driving force of the incarnation.[17] Jesus came freely, but He came with the purpose of dying for our sins and coming back to life for our eternal hope. He and He alone is the

---

 15. More than 22 percent of Christians in a 2009 survey "strongly agreed" Jesus sinned while on earth (*barna.org*).

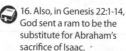 16. Also, in Genesis 22:1-14, God sent a ram to be the substitute for Abraham's sacrifice of Isaac.

 17. *Incarnation* is the term used to describe God becoming human in the Person of Jesus.

SESSION THREE HOLY VOCABULARY

propitiation of our sins, the means by which God's anger and wrath is diverted from us (1 John 2:2). And that makes all the difference in the universe.

Without propitiation, God is against us. With Jesus, He's not only with us, He's for us.

Without propitiation, we are God's enemies. With Jesus, we are at peace with Him forever.

Without propitiation, we are destined to be the eternal recipients of God's glorious wrath. With Jesus, we are destined to be the eternal recipients of His glorious favor.

Without propitiation, we are hopelessly crushed under the weight of our sin. With Jesus, we are wonderfully free to enjoy God forever and ever. Amen.

READ. THINK. DISCUSS.

What are some other examples from film or literature that help illustrate propitiation for you?

If you were asked why understanding propitiation is important, what would you say?

Why do you think Christians don't think very much about this important concept?

How do you know that Jesus was familiar with the doctrine of propitiation?

How is propitiation different from "just being forgiven"?

3.5 REDEMPTION

"To buy back." That's what *redemption* means. Our everyday lives include countless examples of redemption. We redeem coupons, gift certificates, and rain checks, among other things. By its very nature, redemption costs someone something. Redeeming a coupon seems "free" at the store, but someone somewhere took a price cut so you could save money. Economically speaking, there's no such thing as a free lunch. Neither is there a free redemption.

In addition to cost, the concept of redemption involves trading in one thing for something better. After a rain check is redeemed, you have an item or experience you didn't have before the redemption. When a slave is set free, that person is redeemed from one life to another—from servitude to freedom. In both instances, there is a greater sense of good after redemption than before.

Our culture often talks about the redemption of people's lives, but it does so under the assumption that redemption is up to the individual to pursue. We're meant to atone for our cultural errs by doing a better job as humans to help out our fellow humans.

Let's say that you're a drug dealer on the streets of Anytown, U.S.A., who gets caught and sent to prison. While there, you realize your wrongs, so when you get paroled, you want redemption. Our culture would say that one way you could redeem yourself is by working in an afterschool program to keep kids away from the drugs you once sold. That's a fine way to spend your time, but the idea behind it assumes that since you're the source of your problems, it's up to you to make up for the wrong you did. But that's not redemption. At least it's not what the Bible means by redemption.

REDEMPTION'S PRICE TAG

When people in the first century read about "redemption," certain images would have immediately come to mind. For the Greek reader, the word referred to a large amount of money slaves might save up to buy back their own freedom.[18] For the Jewish reader, redemption had roots in the Old Testament. In that context, it was sometimes used to describe the price paid to free a slave,[19] but it also referred to some of God's great acts. For example, the exodus, when the Israelites were brought up out of slavery in Egypt, was described in this way:

> **"Therefore tell the Israelites: I am Yahweh, and I will deliver you from the forced labor of the Egyptians and free you from slavery to them. I will redeem you with an outstretched arm and great acts of judgment" (Exodus 6:6).**

Both images point to one of the key truths about redemption: There is always a price to be

---

 18. Slaves were occasionally paid for their work, and some were able to save enough money over time to buy their way out of slavery.

 19. Both Boaz and Jeremiah act as redeemers. Check out Ruth 4:12 and Jeremiah 32:16-44.

paid. And it's expensive. However, when it comes to our personal redemption, which the New Testament describes, we aren't the ones left to cover the cost. In God's economy, He took care of the price for our redemption with one huge payment. Through the sacrificial death of Jesus on the cross, we're bought back from the slavery of sin and death.

God's redemption has a totality and finality to it. We are redeemed by the precious blood of Christ. The price for our selfish, disobedient break in fellowship with God was paid, and now we get to live forever as His children.

WHAT ARE WE REDEEMED FROM?
To buy us back for God, it cost Jesus His life. Peter put it like this:

> **"For you know that you were redeemed from your empty way of life inherited from the fathers, not with perishable things, like silver or gold, but with the precious blood of Christ, like that of a lamb without defect or blemish" (1 Peter 1:18-19).**

Since Jesus gave His life to buy us back, it is essential that we understand exactly what He rescued us from. Peter said we're redeemed from an "empty way of life." We're also redeemed from sin and death, according to Paul in Romans 8:2. But God's redemption doesn't stop with these, although they would be more than sufficient. According to Galatians 3:13,

> **"Christ has redeemed us from the curse of the law . . ."**

The Galatians 3:10-13 passage is the only place in Paul's writings where the phrase "curse of the law" occurs, and he applies it directly to the subject of redemption. Perhaps Paul had a particular Old Testament passage in mind:

> **"Cursed is anyone who does not put the words of this law into practice" (Deuteronomy 27:26).**

Guilty as charged. How many of us can hold our heads high when looking at Deuteronomy 27? We may not be guilty of breaking a law such as killing a neighbor in secret. But dishonoring a parent? Withholding justice from someone? Not as easy to deny. We don't quite measure up, to say the least. Which means we are cursed.

Right after that verse, the Bible outlines a series of specific blessings for keeping the law and a series of curses for disobedience. The blessings are 14 verses long.[20] Not a bad number of blessings . . . if you stopped reading there. The curses resume in Deuteronomy 28:15 and continue for 53 verses, almost four times as many.

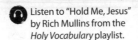 Listen to "Hold Me, Jesus" by Rich Mullins from the *Holy Vocabulary* playlist.

 20. See Deuteronomy 28:1-14 for the specific blessings and 28:15-68 for the curses.

God created a law that only a perfect, sinless person would be able to obey. Did God know such perfection would be impossible for a person to obtain? Yes. Even before creating the law, He knew we would need a Redeemer—a sinless Rescuer willing to go to incredible lengths to buy us back from the curse of the law. And our empty lives. And sin and death.

A FUTURE INHERITANCE

We know that redemption requires a price, which Jesus paid with His blood. Redemption also has an object, which in this case is us. We were the ones bought back, and we are the ones who get to live freely in intimacy with God. But are we the only ones who receive the benefits of redemption? Not exactly. A curious passage in Ephesians 1 leads us to believe Jesus' redemptive act had dual beneficiaries.

Twice in just a few verses of Ephesians 1, Paul described an "inheritance" related to Jesus' redemptive act. The first time he mentions it is in verses 13-14 in connection with the gift of the Holy Spirit.

> "In Him you also, when you heard the word of truth, the gospel of your salvation—in Him when you believed—were sealed with the promised Holy Spirit. *He is the down payment of our inheritance,* for the redemption of the possession, to the praise of His glory" (emphasis added).

The Holy Spirit is sort of like earnest money—God's unbreakable pledge that He will give us all the spiritual riches He has stored up in the heavenlies. Before you get too excited about riches, know that this inheritance isn't monetary. It doesn't have anything to do with health, safety, or comfort. Because of Jesus' redemption, we inherit something better. We inherit God. Our inheritance is the ability and capacity to fully know and enjoy God for all eternity.

But then just a few verses later, Paul wrote:

> "I pray that the eyes of your heart may be enlightened so you may know what is the hope of His calling, what are *the glorious riches of His inheritance* among the saints, and what is the immeasurable greatness of His power to us who believe, according to the working of His vast strength" (Ephesians 1:18-19, emphasis added).

We're not the ones inheriting something in these verses. God is. Paul clearly pointed to God's inheritance, not our inheritance. So what could be so precious as to be called inheritance to the God of the universe—He who has cattle on a thousand hills? He who is perfectly content in and of Himself? He in whom the entire fabric of reality holds together? Us.

Just as our inheritance isn't material but personal, so is the inheritance of God. We are His inheritance. You see the same thing a few verses earlier in Ephesians 1:11:

> "In Him we were also made His inheritance, predestined according to the purpose of the One who works out everything in agreement with the decision of His will . . ." (Ephesians 1:11).

It's unfathomable to think about what Christ did on the cross in buying us back, but He also bought something for God. It's a redemption with a double direction. Jesus' redemption secured both an inheritance for us and for God, and now both we and God wait in expectation to fully inherit each other when we join Him in heaven one day.

READ. THINK. DISCUSS.

In what ways have you experienced the redemption of Jesus in your life?

What was the most meaningful part of examining redemption to you?

What did Christ redeem us from? And what did He redeem us for?

How does it change your life to know that you are the inheritance of God?

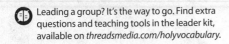
Leading a group? It's the way to go. Find extra questions and teaching tools in the leader kit, available on *threadsmedia.com/holyvocabulary*.

HOLY SPIRIT

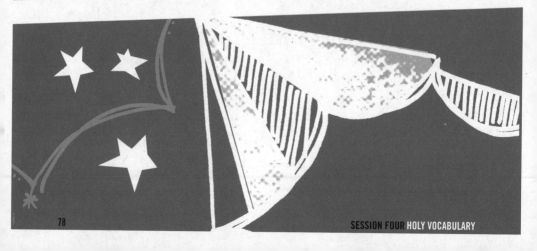

THE GIFT OF THE **HOLY SPIRIT**

Turn on the television in the dark hours of the night and you'll inevitably encounter two things: religious programming and professional wrestling. On one channel, a guy's hit over the head with a chair. Flip to another channel and people are shouting about "the Holy Ghost" and falling down on a stage. An off-the-top-rope body slam on one. Eyes rolling into the backs of people's heads and strange languages being spoken on the other. Watching both programs, you might have the exact same question about each:

Is this for real?

That's a valid question, especially given the fact that some people of faith seem to have a much more intimate association with the Holy Spirit, aka the Holy Ghost, than others. On one extreme end of the spectrum are people who appear to have continuous conversations with someone who no one else can see, hear, or understand. Then at the other end are those who keep the Holy Spirit at arm's distance and ask very little from this promised presence in their lives.

The Holy Spirit is the misunderstood, and often forgotten, member of the Trinity. When we think about the Holy Spirit, we think in terms of mystery, of the strange and borderline paranormal. And it's the Holy Spirit who turns Christians from regular people into raging crazies in the eyes of the world. Rather than fear and confusion, however, the Holy Spirit deserves our reverence and awe. After all, our flight from the Christian subculture rests solely on His shoulders.

Thankfully, to get to know the Holy Spirit and His role in our lives, we don't have to rely on late-night TV programming. In Scripture we find everything from the mysterious to the tangible and logical when it comes to the Spirit of God. The Holy Spirit is God's great gift to the believing community. He's working in us at all times for our good and God's glory. The only question is how aware of His presence we want to be.

4.1 COUNSELOR

Put yourself in the shoes of Jesus' disciples immediately following His death on the cross. That night—when Peter abandoned Jesus and the rest of His friends scattered for cover—was their darkest hour. The man they'd given up their lives to follow was dead. Three days of despair followed before the break of day on Sunday morning, when all of a sudden there was Jesus. Alive, fresh, and smiling. Smiling!

Jesus' resurrection was followed by 40 days of fellowship, intimacy, and learning with Him. The disciples finally understood the true and deeper meaning behind all of Jesus' words and actions. They were en route back to Galilee, a place that held many memories for them, when they ran into Jesus waiting for them on top of a mountain. Having no more qualms or questions about His identity, they fell on their faces and worshiped Him as Lord. And then He spoke to them.[1]

Jesus spoke about His authority, and in light of that authority He gave this band of rejuvenated followers their marching orders. They were to take the message of the gospel far and wide, teaching everyone the glorious news of hope in Jesus' resurrection. And He closed His commission with these words of reassurance:

> **"Remember, I am with you always, to the end of the age"** (Matthew 28:20).

Those were encouraging words, for they remembered what life was like without Jesus. Those three days of questioning, fear, and self-hatred were still fresh on their minds. But those days were over. He would be with them always. Except for the fact that when He got done speaking, He left.[2]

In that moment when the disciples could have stared with open mouths up into heaven, wondering how Jesus' departure squared with His promise to be with them always, they did nothing of the sort. Mark recorded in His gospel that after the ascension of Jesus into heaven:

> **"They went out and preached everywhere . . ."** (Mark 16:20).

Evidently the disciples weren't shocked or surprised at His departure; if they were, it certainly didn't deter them from moving forward with the Great Commission. Perhaps there was even a tinge of excitement mingled with sadness as they watched Jesus ascend into the heavens above.

SIDE BY SIDE WITH THE SPIRIT

The disciples knew they could take Jesus at His word, and He told them the day would come when He would send them His replacement of sorts:

---

 1. John describes the disciples' encounter with the risen Christ in chapters 20 and 21 of his Gospel.

 2. *"Then after speaking to them, the Lord Jesus was taken up into heaven and sat down at the right hand of God"* (Mark 16:19).

> "I will ask the Father, and He will give you another Counselor to be with you forever. He is the Spirit of truth. The world is unable to receive Him because it doesn't see Him or know Him. But you do know Him, because He remains with you and will be in you" (John 14:16-17).

The Holy Spirit is Jesus' answer to the needs of God's children. He's the One who is here in Jesus' absence to walk with us through life. In the John 14 passage, Jesus refers to the Holy Spirit as our "Counselor," from the Greek word *paraclete*. *Paraclete* is based on a combination of two words: *para*, meaning "by the side," and *kaleo* meaning "to call." The *paraclete*, then, is one who has been called to the side of another.

"The side," though, isn't a description of proximity but of relationship. The Holy Spirit doesn't walk side by side with us literally. It's better than that. As Christ-followers, the Holy Spirit dwells within us. He's by our side in the sense that He's on our side.

While He was on earth, Jesus committed a lot of time to His relationships, especially with His disciples. When He ascended to heaven, the Holy Spirit picked up those relationships where Jesus left off. As Jesus had promised,

> "The Counselor, the Holy Spirit . . . will teach you all things and remind you of everything I have told you" (John 14:26).

In the same way, the Spirit continues in relationship with Christ-followers today. He is committed to relationship with us until Jesus returns.[3]

EVERYBODY NEEDS AN ADVOCATE

When we think about the Holy Spirit as Counselor, it doesn't just mean someone who gives us advice. The Holy Spirit doesn't give advice, for advice is based on opinion and can either be accepted or rejected. He's not the Spirit of suggestion; He's the Spirit of truth. You can be sure that when the Holy Spirit speaks, He's not giving us information we're meant to take into account in our decision; He's telling us the truth, and our response should be obedience.

A better way to think of the Counselor is in a legal context. *Paraclete* was used by Greek writers to speak of a legal advisor, one who would come forward on behalf of and as the representative of another.[4] The Counselor is a divine helper, our advocate. Indeed, the Holy Spirit is the greatest help for followers of Jesus.

It's one thing if someone wants to help you but doesn't have the resources to do so. In that case, the help is really not much more than a sympathetic ear or a shoulder to cry on. Not so with the Holy Spirit. The Holy Spirit, far from a benign presence, is Jesus' personal representative on earth. He speaks (Acts 1:16), teaches (John 14:26), testifies (John 15:26),

---

 3. Thirty-eight percent of Christians in a 2009 Barna Group study "strongly agreed" that the Holy Spirit doesn't exist (*barna.org*).

 4. Think: Atticus Finch's legal representation of wrongfully accused Tom Robinson in *To Kill a Mockingbird*.

"searches" (1 Corinthians 2:10), and even "intercedes" for us (Romans 8:26-27). In fact, we owe every bit of our spiritual development and power to the work of the Holy Spirit in our lives.

EVIDENCE OF THE SPIRIT IN SCRIPTURE

John 14 isn't the first time the Holy Spirit shows up in Scripture. He pops up now and again throughout the Old Testament. The Spirit was present with God for the creation of the world:

> "Now the earth was formless and empty, darkness covered the surface of the watery depths, and the Spirit of God was hovering over the surface of the waters" (Genesis 1:2).

He was with Bezalel, filling and enabling him to work with his hands to construct the sanctuary of God:

> "Moses then said to the Israelites: 'Look, the LORD has appointed by name Bezalel son of Uri, son of Hur, of the tribe of Judah. He has filled him with God's Spirit, with wisdom, understanding, and ability in every kind of craft'" (Exodus 35:30-31).

The Holy Spirit descended upon Saul, and he began to prophesy:[5]

> "So he went to Naioth in Ramah. The Spirit of God also came on him, and as he walked along, he prophesied until he entered Naioth in Ramah" (1 Samuel 19:23).

And He made His presence known periodically throughout the Book of Judges, giving God's appointed people the strength to defeat enemies with things like jawbones of donkeys.[6] But starting in the Book of Acts, the Holy Spirit showed up like never before.

In Acts 2, the Holy Spirit didn't come alongside an individual. This time He descended upon the entire community of Christians. From that day forward, as Jesus promised, the Spirit wasn't an occasional visitor but a permanent resident, dwelling within everyone who believes in Jesus.

Given His vital importance, we can't help but wonder why the Holy Spirit is ignored in some Christian circles and not treated with the reverence and awe He deserves in others. Our misunderstanding of and lack of experience with the Holy Spirit is visible in the simple fact that most of us refer to Him as "it" when we talk.

----

 5. As a result of his prophesying, Saul collapsed naked before Samuel. Interesting.

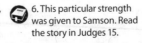 6. This particular strength was given to Samson. Read the story in Judges 15.

But the Holy Spirit isn't an "it." He's a "He." And as long as our misunderstanding and fear of Him motivates us to keep Him an arm's length away, we will live lives of spiritual lethargy and fail to live up to our full potential as God's light in our world.

We never, ever, ever have to pray for God to be with us. He's already here and, as Jesus promised, will be with us forever. Because He's here as our Advocate, we can be assured that He's not only with us—He's *for* us. For our good. For our development as followers of Christ. For our continued growth in godliness. Thank God for that.

READ. THINK. DISCUSS.

What are the top three words that come to mind when you think of the Holy Spirit?

What do those words reveal about your general attitude toward Him?

Why do you think so little attention is paid to the Holy Spirit in church circles?

What are some practical ways you can try to become more aware of the Holy Spirit's presence and voice in your life?

How is your relationship with God impacted by knowing the Holy Spirit is with you always to act as your Counselor?

What's the difference in knowing God is "with" you or "for" you?

4.2 FRUIT

What do the first chapter of the Bible and the last chapter of the Bible have in common? Fruit, for one thing. On the third day of creation, God created vegetation:

> "Seed-bearing plants according to their kinds and trees bearing fruit with seed in it, according to their kinds. And God saw that it was good" (Genesis 1:12).

Then in the final chapter of the Bible, the apostle John recounts the following from his vision of what's to come:

> "Then he showed me the river of living water, sparkling like crystal, flowing from the throne of God and of the Lamb down the middle of the broad street of the city. On both sides of the river was the tree of life bearing 12 kinds of fruit, producing its fruit every month. The leaves of the tree are for healing the nations, and there will no longer be any curse" (Revelation 22:1-3).

Similar references are found throughout Scripture as well. The culture at the time the Bible was written was primarily agrarian, so we shouldn't be surprised by so many references to fruit within the biblical text.[7]

In the Old Testament, fruit was a part of the sacrificial offering (Leviticus 19:23-25). Fruitful harvest is a sign of God's blessing (Leviticus 26:3-4), while the lack of fruit is part of the curse for disobedience (Leviticus 26:18-20). But fruit is also an enduring metaphor throughout the Bible meant to convey people's actions, both good and bad. When you think about it, "fruit" is a very appropriate way to describe that.

Fruit doesn't determine the kind of tree it comes from. Rather, fruit is the evidence of the nature of the tree on which it grows. For example, an apple tree isn't an apple tree because it produces apples; it produces apples because it's an apple tree. I know that's a simple concept, but it's imperative in grasping what fruit represents in the biblical context and how that relates to the Holy Spirit. Metaphorically, the fruits (actions) we produce are rooted in the people we are deep down inside. It's the Holy Spirit's job to make us people who produce the right kind of fruit.

THE FRUIT OF THE SPIRIT

One of the most famous Bible passages about the Holy Spirit is found in Galatians 5:22-23:

> "But the fruit of the Spirit is love, joy, peace, patience, kindness, goodness, faith, gentleness, self-control. Against such things there is no law."

7. Read Margaret Feinberg's *Scouting the Divine* for a more in-depth look at agrarian metaphors in Scripture.

Ah, the fruit of the Spirit. I'm singing the song in my head right now.[8] We could spend days on each specific attribute of the Christian life described in these verses, and that would be a worthy pursuit. But for the sake of this discussion, let's simply ask one question: Why are these characteristics called "fruit"? They could just as easily be called "benefits" or "works."

"Works of the Spirit" might seem to fit, especially given that the Spirit is working in us all the time. But if you look at the context of Galatians 5, you'll see that Paul preceded His statement about the fruit of the Spirit with comments on the "works of the flesh"—things such as sexual immorality, idolatry, and jealousy (Galatians 5:19-21).

These two lists appear back to back in Paul's letter, which leads us to assume he intended to make a distinction between the *works* of the flesh and the *fruit* of the Spirit.

WORKS VERSUS FRUIT

So what is that distinction? Well for starters, works are based solely on our effort. We exert a certain amount of energy in the hopes of producing a certain outcome. Some works take a lot of exertion, others not so much. But regardless of the degree, it's still effort on our part.

It's tempting for us to look at a list like the one in Galatians 5:22-23 and think, *God is telling me to do good things. To work at being loving, patient, good, and faithful.* That might be a noble sentiment, but it totally misses the emphasis placed on the word "fruit." God isn't interested in people who put forth the effort to do good things; He's interested in people who are, at the very core of their being, good people.

That's what the biblical metaphor of fruit is all about. Just as edible fruit is a reflection of the kind of tree it's on, so it is with people. The fruit of the Spirit is the natural expression of who we are as children of God. Jesus explains this for us in Matthew 12.[9]

Finally fed up with the disparaging remarks of the Pharisees, it's as if Jesus spins on His heels and counters: "Pharisees, would you like to know what your real problem is? Some might say it's that you lie. Or that you steal. Or that you lust or tie heavy burdens on men's backs. But those are all symptoms. And you can try to clean up your behavior if you want to, but that doesn't solve the problem. The problem is you're the wrong kind of tree."

Jesus continued, saying essentially: "If you have an orange tree in your backyard, but you like apples, the solution to the problem isn't to rip all the oranges off the tree. They'll come back eventually. Neither is the solution to go and pick some apples and staple them to the branches of the tree. The solution is to dig up the old tree, throw it away, and plant an apple tree in its place."

8. Don't know this song? YouTube it. Consider yourself warned, though. It will stick in your head like "It's a Small World."

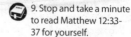
9. Stop and take a minute to read Matthew 12:33-37 for yourself.

The implication for the Pharisees was that they might be able to will themselves (or work themselves) to stop cheating, lying, or stealing. But ultimately, those are only temporary bandages that don't address the deep, underlying issue. The real issue was their hearts—and the Pharisees had the wrong kind. The fruit only reflects what's at the root of the tree.

BECOMING NEW TREES

We learn this truth little by little as we grow into the people we were made to be. Take me, for example. I like to make lists. Almost obsessively. I like to know how much money is in my checking account at any given moment. I like to print my itinerary when I travel. I like to have every appointment calendared so I know what's coming. That's who I am. A nerd.

But a few years ago, I was tempted by the elusive call of "cool." So I scratched one thing off my regular to-do list: getting a haircut. For months, I grew the hair. Long. I wanted it to wisp over my eyes like a rock star. I searched high and low for the right consistency of hair gel that would make it look naturally messy, in just the right way.

For a number of months I placed myself in bondage like this. Each day, wondering whether or not my hair was falling just right. Whether it was the right consistency. And then one day I did something incredibly freeing. I got it cut.

Ahhhh . . .

My sense of relief came, I think, because that little act was a sign of something bigger. It was an example of me accepting who I am. I am a short haircut guy. It fits my personality. Such is the case with the fruit of the Spirit. Sure, we have to try and be loving and patient and joyful and all the rest. But our trying isn't works. Nor is it burdensome and strenuous, or a fight against our nature. We aren't trying to become something different. We're trying to step aside and allow the Holy Spirit to develop His fruit in our lives so we can fully embrace who we already are in Him.

Salvation is about the Holy Spirit entering your life with a cosmic backhoe, digging up the tree of your heart, and planting a new one in its place. And the new tree bears fruit. Fruit like love, joy, peace, patience, kindness, goodness, faith, gentleness, and self-control.

See it? The fruit is the expression of the person the Holy Spirit has made you to be in Christ. His work in your life is to encourage and bring out the righteousness of Christ already inside of you. That's what fruit is.

Not fruits, but fruit. These aren't the fruits of the Spirit; these characteristics aren't meant to be isolated from each other. You and I don't get to pick and choose which ones we want like food from a cafeteria line. They're a total package.

Watch the *Holy Vocabulary* video "Holy Spirit (hō′lē spir′it) *n*." with your group or at *threadsmedia.com/holyvocabulary*.

No one, after they've flown off the handle, can justifiably claim, "I'm just not a patient person." We can't hide behind our personalities as an excuse, for the truth is, in Christ, we are patient people. We are loving people. We are kind, good, and faithful too. This fruit is the outward expression of who we are in Christ. The only question is how much are we willing to yield to that work of the Holy Spirit as He brings out these characteristics inside of us?

That's the difference between works and fruit, between doing and being. We don't "do" the fruit of the Spirit. The fruit of the Spirit reflects our new root in Christ, and we accept that we are people who embody it. The Holy Spirit is about transforming us into the image of Christ, and if you look closely at the list in Galatians 5:22-23, you find a great description of One person who embodied all these characteristics. May we accept that we've become people who embody them too.

READ. THINK. DISCUSS.

How does calling these characteristics "fruit," instead of "works," change how you think about your relationship with the Holy Spirit?

Where do you see the Holy Spirit bringing out these characteristics in your life? How have you experienced Him doing so?

Is it a challenge for you to not try to make the fruit into works? Explain.

Do you think you'll ever perfectly embody the fruit of the Holy Spirit? Why or why not?

4.3 SANCTIFY

In his book, *Just Like Jesus*, Max Lucado attempts a two-sentence summation of a big Christian truth. He states: "God loves you just the way you are, but he refuses to leave you that way. He wants you to be just like Jesus."[10]

In a great little nutshell, that's what it means to be sanctified—becoming more like Jesus. It's what happens in the meantime, between when you became a Christian and when you join Jesus in God's presence in heaven.

Here's a more technical definition of *sanctification* to help us unpack a challenging concept: "The work of God's free grace, whereby we are renewed in the whole man after the image of God, and are enabled more and more to die unto sin, and live unto righteousness."[11]

God's plan for your life isn't that you just pray a prayer and sit back, waiting to get into heaven someday. The Christian experience is one of constant spiritual development and change. The Holy Spirit molds and forms you so that in character, motivation, and action you resemble Jesus more and more.

CUT OFF YOUR BOOTSTRAPS

Don't miss the critical role the Holy Spirit plays in your sanctification. It is His job to make you more like Jesus. We couldn't do it on our own. The temptation for Christians is, and has always been, to look at this process of becoming more like Jesus with a "bootstraps" approach. That is, we decide we're going to grit our teeth and pull ourselves up by our bootstraps as we try hard to do the right thing. And frankly, that's exactly the attitude Paul seems to be advocating in Philippians 2:12:

> **"So then, my dear friends, just as you have always obeyed, not only in my presence, but now even more in my absence, work out your own salvation with fear and trembling."**

Great. That sounds fun. And it also sounds like a life of frustration and defeat. I can't count the number of promises I've made and broken to God about trying to stop doing this or start doing that. In my own life—and I believe in the lives of many other Christ-followers—I've tried so hard to be godly and failed so many times at doing so that I'm tempted to walk around with my head hung low in defeat.

In that light sanctification sounds awful, and Paul's words aren't very encouraging. The verb tense in verse 12 indicates a sense of working at something continuously and unceasingly until it is accomplished. Perhaps you've worked at being Christ-like with a similar drive up to this point, yet still feel defeated. Surely it would be easier if God

---

10. Max Lucado, *Just Like Jesus* (Nashville: Thomas Nelson, Inc., 2003), 3.

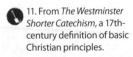 11. From *The Westminster Shorter Catechism*, a 17th-century definition of basic Christian principles.

simply saved us and sent us on our way, saying, "Good luck! Be good!" But He doesn't, and thankfully Paul didn't stop with verse 12.

Immediately after telling us to continuously work out our own salvation until it's complete, Paul wrote this:

> **"For it is God who is working in you, enabling you both to will and to act for His good purpose" (Philippians 2:13).**

That's good news. We are reminded that the Holy Spirit is at work within us. But I'll be the first to admit Paul's a little confusing here.

I like verse 13 more than verse 12. I like the thought of placing my burden on God, and I like the promise that God's working in me, not me working on my own. He's the one who is continuing to keep me in His grace and will carry me through this process of justification, sanctification, and ultimately into glorification. This reality makes sanctification God's work, not mine. But it's confusing that the statements "work out your own salvation" and "it is God who is working in you" are in the same book of the Bible, not to mention in back-to-back sentences.

Paul's statements seem contradictory. Logic tells us that God's work replaces our work. Because He works, we don't have to. And to some extent that is true, isn't it? Because Christ was righteous, our righteousness is taken care of. Because Christ died for our sins, we don't have to. Because Christ was sinless, we are declared innocent. So how does our work and God's work come together in our sanctification? Reconciling the two has great implications for how we live—and how we don't live.

HAVING FAITH IN WHO WE ALREADY ARE

To understand what it means for both us and God to have active roles in our becoming like Christ, let's first look at what it doesn't mean. Paul wasn't referring to spending time and energy working to become something different. The wonderful truth of the gospel is that we *have already* become something different. In Christ, the old is gone and the new is come, for any person who is in Christ "is a new creation" (2 Corinthians 5:17).

In sanctification, it's not as if we are willing ourselves to change into something we're not. Instead, because we have been made new through Christ's work and the power of the Holy Spirit, we are moment-by-moment embracing who we truly are.

To put it another way, we are bringing our external actions into conformity with our inner reality. On the inside, in the deepest parts of who we are, we are the sons and daughters of God. The righteousness of Christ. Saints. That's our identity; our

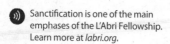

Sanctification is one of the main emphases of the L'Abri Fellowship. Learn more at *labri.org*.

fundamental definition as saved people. But there are many areas of our lives that haven't caught up yet. Sure, our hearts have been changed, but there are still those pieces of the person we used to be hanging on with white knuckles. That's where the work comes in, because we're in a continual fight to pry those hands loose.

Paul described it this way in Galatians 5:16-17:

> "I say then, walk by the Spirit and you will not carry out the desire of the flesh. For the flesh desires what is against the Spirit, and the Spirit desires what is against the flesh; these are opposed to each other, so that you don't do what you want."

The conflict is real. The battle is ongoing. And everyone who has seriously sought to attack the sin in their lives and run hard after God can attest to the violence of the internal struggle. But understanding that through the power of the Holy Spirit and the death and resurrection of Jesus we have been made new changes the nature of the "work" we're doing.

Because of that newness, every time we faithfully choose godliness and deny sin, we're actually choosing to embrace our new identity. Conversely, when we choose to sin, it's as if we're putting on a mask and acting like someone different than who we really are. When we work, we're working to be the true us. The "born again" us. And we're working hard to believe that God is at work in us, that He can conform us through the Holy Spirit to the image of Christ, and that He has freed us from being slaves to sin.[12] That's the role we play in our sanctification process. Being faithful to who we are in Him.

God's work, on the other hand, is the execution of the conforming, transforming, and changing within us. While we work to have faith in who we are as God's redeemed children and to act in a manner that reflects that, God's busy doing the actual prying of those white-knuckled fingers from around our hearts. Sanctification is about work—the work of God in us, and our work to have faith in His ability to do that work.

Once again, we find faith as the central work of the Christian. What about you? Do you believe what the Bible says about you? That you're a saint? A son? A daughter? The righteousness of Christ? Work hard at believing these things to be true. Work hard at believing you've been transformed.

While you're working hard to believe, the Holy Spirit is working hard, too. He's busy sanctifying you, prying the remnants of who you used to be out of the grasp of the child of God you are now. He's working hard to transform you into who you've already become in Christ.

---

 12. For another biblical example of this principle, check out John 6:28-29. Jesus summed up the work of God in this: believing.

READ. THINK. DISCUSS.

What did you think sanctification meant before reading this section? Did you think you had to do all the work? Explain.

How do you think our work and God's work at sanctification fit together?

How does knowing your true identity in Christ change the way you view sanctification?

What's the difference between working hard and working hard at believing?

What is one area of your life in which you need to work hard at believing?

4.4 FILLED

"Be filled with the Spirit" (Ephesians 5:18).

While this is a nice idea, it's more complicated than it sounds. Few statements, concepts, or doctrines have divided the church to a greater degree than the interpretation of what it means to be filled with the Holy Spirit.

Some people believe that being filled with the Spirit is about losing control, much like the apostles lost control in Acts 2.[13] Along similar lines is the argument that being filled with the Spirit has clear, physical manifestations that go along with it, most notably, speaking in tongues (un-understandable languages). Then there are others who claim that being filled with the Spirit is really just a fancy way of saying "obedient."

So to better understand what Paul meant when he told the church at Ephesus to "be filled with the Spirit," let's start by considering what we know to be true.

A GRAMMAR LESSON

First of all, we know the Holy Spirit is given as a gift to all who follow Christ. In the Book of Acts, the presence of the Holy Spirit was the authenticating mark for new believers.[14] Their question wasn't, "Has that guy prayed the sinner's prayer?"[15] or "Did we capture his information on a perspective church membership card?" Instead it was, "Did she receive the gift of the Holy Spirit?" The presence of the Holy Spirit in someone's life was the stamp of God's approval and the verification that his or her salvation was indeed legit.

But here's where it starts to get complicated. Ephesians was written to the church—those who were already Christ-followers, and therefore those who already had the Holy Spirit living inside them. The very fact that Paul told them to be filled with the Spirit indicates that it's possible to have the Holy Spirit inside you but not *be filled* with Him.

And then there's another problem. The verb tense of "be filled" in Ephesians 5:18 reveals it's describing both something you're supposed to do and something that's supposed to be done to you. First of all, this verse is a command: "Be filled with the Spirit." A command is, by its very nature, something you're supposed to do:

> **"Don't commit adultery" (Exodus 20:14).**
> **"Flee from sexual immorality" (1 Corinthians 6:18).**
> **"Devote yourselves to prayer" (Colossians 4:2).**

The problem is, the "be filled" command is in the passive voice. Just a quick grammar refresher here: The active voice is the verb tense used when describing something you're

---

 13. This happened on the Day of Pentecost—aka the Feast of Weeks—one of the three main Jewish holidays.

 14. For examples, check out Acts 4:8; 4:31; 7:55; 9:17; 13:9; and 13:52.

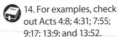 15. Evangelist Billy Graham helped make this confessional prayer (*Dear God, I know that I'm a sinner…*) popular.

supposed to actively do. The passive voice is used when something is done to you. It's the difference between, "Kill that spider," and, "Spider, be killed." Paul challenges us with a biblical command that's supposed to be done to us.

A THING OR TWO ABOUT BOATS

How does this passive command work? It helps me to think of it in terms of an analogy involving various kinds of boats.

Think first about a rowboat. A rowboat is active in nature. The distance you travel in a rowboat is linked exclusively to your effort. If you can pull those oars enough times, you can travel all the way across the ocean. But if you get tired, the forward movement stops.[16]

That's way different than a bass boat. A bass boat is built for speed. You turn the key, the motor tumbles to life, and away you go. No effort is required on your part; all you do is hold onto the steering wheel for dear life.[17]

The Christian life often looks a lot like one of these two circumstances. Rowboat Christians are the ones who believe their spiritual lives are exclusively about effort. They try and try and try to be good Christians, but before they know it, they're exhausted. You can't fault them for their effort. When the time comes that they actually do stop a pattern of sin or establish a pattern of godliness, though, they really have to fight the sense of pride that comes along with it. They're the ones holding the oars, so it's their victory and theirs alone.

At the other extreme are those Christians who want to just "let go and let God." They don't think there is any effort required of them in the Christian experience, so they don't try hard at anything. Sure, we may commend them for their level of faith, but more than likely their lives are devoid of personal discipline and commitment to that faith.

"Be filled with the Spirit" fits in neither category. It's somewhere in the middle. Because it's a passive command, we have a critical role to play in our being filled, but we're also dependent on something—more like Someone—else.

We're not supposed to live like the rowboat where the result depends exclusively on our muscles. We're also not to live like the bass boat, where we just turn the key and enjoy the ride. In terms of boats, the best analogy for the Christian life is the sailboat.

Several factors contribute to the movement of a sailboat. First, the sail must be released in order for the wind to push it along. The speed of the water current also plays a big part in the boat's motion. With these two factors in order, the boat's hull follows along. The sailor's job is to position the sail accurately, depending on the way the wind is blowing. This maneuver, called tacking, helps the sailor keep control of the wind. If the wind and

 16. To find out how fast (or slow!) you could row, use a physics equation like the one found at *sciencebits.com/rowers*.

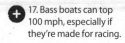 17. Bass boats can top 100 mph, especially if they're made for racing.

the water are calmly moving in the same direction and speed, then the work required of the sailor is minimal.[18]

The forward motion of a sailboat is based exclusively on catching the wind. No wind, no motion. You can't control the wind. You can, however, control the sail. Your job as the sailor is to tie the sail correctly. You point the boat in the right direction and raise the sail up the mast. You judge the conditions around you and make the necessary effort so that when the wind does blow, you're ready to sail.

YIELDING CONTROL

I think the same principle applies to the Christian's role in being filled with the Spirit. We don't fill ourselves with the Spirit. But we do make ourselves available to be filled. We can choose obedience in the little areas of our lives. We can spend time meditating on the Word of God. We can practice the spiritual disciplines.[19] We can pray. We can fast. We can do all of these things and more. When we take this kind of an active role, we're raising the sail and readying the boat. God's wind takes over from there.

Being filled with the Spirit is really about yielding control. We set the conditions, trust in the Holy Spirit, and surrender control to Him. That's why in Ephesians 5 the filling of the Spirit is contrasted to drunkenness:

> "So don't be foolish, but understand what the Lord's will is. And don't get drunk with wine, which leads to reckless actions, but be filled with the Spirit" (Ephesians 5:17-18).

Abusing alcohol yields a person's self control and judgment to the negative effects of the alcohol. But being filled with the Spirit yields the direction of our lives to God and His control. That's His will for your life.

Being filled with the Spirit should be the normative condition for the Christian life. When we're filled with the Spirit, we're recognizing the rule of Jesus over every part of ourselves. We're recognizing that He's in charge of our daily appointments, our money, and even where we eat lunch. When we're filled with the Spirit, our spiritual senses are on high alert, and we remain on the lookout for any opportunity God throws in our path to do good for the sake of the gospel.

According to what Paul wrote in the verses leading up to Ephesians 5:17-18, the filling of the Spirit is linked pretty directly to this kind of spiritual awareness:

> "Pay careful attention, then, to how you walk—not as unwise people but as wise—making the most of the time, because the days are evil" (Ephesians 5:15-16).

---

18. Adapted from *sailing.about.com*.

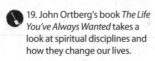 19. John Ortberg's book *The Life You've Always Wanted* takes a look at spiritual disciplines and how they change our lives.

Following these verses, Paul told us that God's will is for us to be filled with the Holy Spirit. Do you see the link? Those filled with the Spirit are very careful about how they walk. But the carefulness isn't a defensive carefulness; it's an offensive one.

When you walk defensively, each step you take is a cautious one. You nervously tread your way through life, because you don't want to get any sin on your shoes. But when you walk through life offensively, you walk with boldness and confidence, always looking for opportunities to share and live out the gospel. You are, in short, very spiritually aware.

So we raise our sails. Day after day. Time and time again. With every decision we make. And then we trust the Holy Spirit (which incidentally, means "divine wind" in Greek) to blow through and fill them up. Only God knows where we go from there.

READ. THINK. DISCUSS.

In what contexts have you heard the phrase "filled with the Spirit"?

What do you think someone who is filled with the Spirit looks like or acts like?

Why do you think God wants that for us? Why is being filled with the Spirit God's will for our lives?

How do you think your normal schedule would be impacted if you were filled with the Spirit?

4.5 GIFTS

My kids love getting gifts. (I guess that whole "blessed is the giver" thing hasn't caught on yet.) My son likes Legos®, light sabers, and baseball bats. He could care less about getting clothes. In a big stack of presents, he'll open a package of socks, nod politely, and then quickly throw them aside in search of a new action figure.

But my little girl? Well, clothes are an entirely different story with her. She'll open her socks and squeal with glee. She doesn't see clothes as a necessary evil that has to be dealt with every morning; she sees them as something to be used and enjoyed. In fact, after she opens up her socks, it's only a matter of time before she's walking awkwardly around having grown by about four inches because she's put them all on at the same time. The value of a gift has everything to do with the perspective of the one receiving it, as my kids' very different responses to clothing gifts demonstrates.

A gift is understood to be a "favor or item bestowed on someone."[20] The term "spiritual gifts" has become synonymous with the specific ways Christians are equipped to do God's work, including everything from preaching to being naturally hospitable. When it comes to our spiritual giftedness, the Holy Spirit is the one doing the bestowing, and we should consider ourselves blessed to be the recipients.

But it's a sad fact that many of us treat the gifts of the Holy Spirit like a little boy opening up a package of socks; they're great to have, but we're looking for something else. Something with value. Something to be played with. Perhaps that's the reason many of us acknowledge that the Holy Spirit gifts individual Christians, but we in reality have no idea how He's gifted us or how to employ the gifts we know we have.

TO EACH HIS OWN

When the Holy Spirit invaded our lives at the moment of salvation, He came bearing gifts for us. If you are a Christian, you have been gifted by the Holy Spirit. There are no exceptions to this rule. Despite what we might see when we look in the mirror, we are, in Christ, gifted individuals.

A few key places in the New Testament detail these gifts of the Spirit. In 1 Corinthians 12, Paul acknowledged the great diversity of spiritual gifts:

> "Now there are different gifts, but the same Spirit. There are different ministries, but the same Lord. And there are different activities, but the same God is active in everyone and everything. A manifestation of the Spirit is given to each person to produce what is beneficial" (1 Corinthians 12:4-7).

---

20. *Holman Illustrated Bible Dictionary* (Nashville: Holman Bible Publishers, 2003), 650.

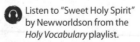 Listen to "Sweet Holy Spirit" by Newworldson from the *Holy Vocabulary* playlist.

He goes on to discuss the specific gifts of wisdom, knowledge, faith, healing, performing miracles, prophecy, discernment, tongues, and the interpretation of tongues before concluding:

> **"But one and the same Spirit is active in all these, distributing to each one as He wills" (1 Corinthians 12:11).**

Based on this passage, we can conclude a few things. First of all, no person is gifted by accident. The Spirit of God is very intentional in choosing what to bestow on whom. The dispersal of gifts isn't done at random or haphazardly; it's done with very specific and individualized intent.

Furthermore, because the other lists of spiritual gifts (Ephesians 4 and Romans 12) don't match this one, we can conclude that these lists are meant to be representative, not exhaustive. Just because a gift doesn't explicitly appear on this list doesn't mean it's not valid. And even the ones that do appear on these lists are exercised in different ways.

For example, two individuals might be gifted to preach the gospel. But they're not going to sound the same when they do. They won't use the same words, and they probably won't even have the same style of preaching. In God's commitment to diversity, we see that somehow the Holy Spirit mingles His gifts with an individual's personality and life experiences to produce an entirely unique outpouring of those gifts. This is yet another example of how God refuses to be limited, and another encouragement for us of His intricate and specific care and provision for His people.

BLESSED TO BE A BLESSING

Accepting the gifts God gives us is the easy part. Who doesn't love getting gifts? But if we're going to be the beneficiaries of spiritual gifts, it would profit us to ask the question of why. Why does the Holy Spirit give us these gifts?

To answer that, let's look at another passage regarding spiritual gifts:

> **"Therefore, brothers, by the mercies of God, I urge you to present your bodies as a living sacrifice, holy and pleasing to God; this is your spiritual worship. Do not be conformed to this age, but be transformed by the renewing of your mind, so that you may discern what is the good, pleasing, and perfect will of God" (Romans 12:1-2).**

A few verses later, Paul includes another list of specific examples of gifts. But at first glance, verses 1 and 2 don't seem to have anything to do with that. To get at how these verses relate to the gifts of the Holy Spirit, let's have a little grammar lesson. Some nouns in the

 Curious how the Spirit's gifted you? Take the spiritual gifts assessment found at *threadsmedia.com/spiritualgifts.*

text above are singular and some are plural. "Mercies," for example, is plural. And who can argue with that?

Paul just spent the first 11 glorious chapters of Romans talking about the depravity of mankind—how we were all hopelessly lost. But then God stepped into our lives, taking His enemies and making them His children. Definitely plural. The mercies of God are innumerable. From the drawing of another breath each morning to our glorious homecoming in heaven, the mercies of God abound.

Let's keep going. In light of God's mercies (plural), we should offer our bodies (plural) as a living sacrifice (singular). Sacrifice, not sacrifices. Many bodies, one sacrifice. And the absence of that "s," that one little letter, makes all the difference in the world.

When I think of a sacrifice to God, I think of the Old Testament. I think of blood and an altar. And animals. I imagine ropes being tied around the legs of a goat or bull or lamb. Then that animal is forcibly hauled onto the altar and a priest stands over it. Then the sacrifice is made and offered to God.

That's an example of a daily, individual sacrifice made to atone for specific sins. We might look at Romans 12:1-2 and apply a similar picture. Every morning you and I choose whose agenda we will follow that day. We stand at the fork in the road of obedience or disobedience, and we choose whether we will live for ourselves—our pleasure, our satisfaction, our bank accounts, and our comfort—or for God. If we choose the latter, then we metaphorically place ourselves on the altar before Him each day. We spread our arms open wide in a gesture of absolute submission. We invite Him to do as He wills with us. We have chosen for that day to make ourselves fully and completely at the disposal of God.

The idea of a daily, living, individual sacrifice is certainly in the Bible.[21] It came straight from the mouth of the Lord Jesus. And though Paul absolutely lived out that call, proving through trials and beatings and hardships and difficulties that he was a sacrifice, that's not the exact idea present in Romans 12. If it were, Paul would have challenged us to daily make ourselves "living sacrifices." Plural. Each one of us. Every day. Lots of sacrifices.

But there's no "s." Romans 12 isn't about individuals; it describes a group project. We are to corporately come together in the church with everything we have—all our talents, gifts, and resources—and offer one sacrifice. God's will is that we become participants in the wonderful group project of the church.

That's why the Holy Spirit has gifted us as individuals. Not so that we might profit financially or build our own reputation in any way, but to give ourselves for the good of others and the building up of the body of Christ.

---

 21. See Luke 9:23 for an example of this daily individual sacrifice.

We are blessed in order to be a blessing; not to hoard the blessing for ourselves. Regardless of what you see when you look in the mirror, be convinced of this: The Holy Spirit has gone to great lengths to find the perfect gifts for you. And He's given it to you with the expectation that you would learn to use it in conjunction with your personality for the good of others, the building up of the church, and ultimately the glory of Jesus.

See, when you aren't exercising your spiritual gifts—or when you don't even know what they are—you're doing more than robbing yourself of the great joy of serving Jesus. You're also robbing the rest of the church. The church can't be what it's supposed to be until you are willing to be who you're supposed to be.

The church is meant to be a group project—a corporate sacrifice—where individuals serve in the specific ways in which the Holy Spirit has gifted them. But way too many of us see the church as a place where we're supposed to soak like sponges, rather than give ourselves fully. But now we're talking about the church. And the church has some words that need rescuing, too . . .

READ. THINK. DISCUSS.

What are your spiritual gifts? How do you know?

In what capacity are you using those gifts?

Why do you think Romans 12 describes the exercise of your spiritual gifts as God's will for your life?

Do you think most people have a good knowledge of how they have been gifted? Why or why not?

CHURCH

SESSION FIVE HOLY VOCABULARY

ARE YOU COMMITTED TO THE CHURCH?

Now here's a subject with some baggage. Throughout history people have blamed Christians for many things. Wars, racism, impeding the progress of science, and forced conversion, just to name a few. Sadly, church history confirms that such claims have some basis in reality. Perhaps that's why the church has embarked on a serious marketing campaign in recent years.

In lieu of such strong accusations and misunderstandings, Christians have reevaluated everything about church, from the color of carpet to the use of video screens to the style of music. All of this is an effort to help people see past the negative opinions—whether justified or unjustified—they have of the church.

Adjustments like these and others have caused an interesting side effect: The church is going through an identity crisis. As a whole, the church no longer knows what it is. And individual church congregations aren't sure if they're evangelical, emerging, traditional, seeker-friendly, elder- or staff-led, non-denominational, missional, or home-based . . . to name a few options. Maybe it's time we step back from the comfort of our churches and ask ourselves the question, "How does today's church line up with God's design for it?"

That's a pretty important question, especially considering the church is the only organization in the history of the universe with the endorsement of God Almighty. Jesus never promised to build a social organization or a parachurch ministry. He never threw His weight behind a political system or a needs-based nonprofit. For that reason, if for none other, we can't abandon the church, no matter how dysfunctional it's become.

The church is the bride and body of Christ. It's the community of called-out believers on mission for God. It's the saints of God, the salt of the earth, and the hope for the world. The church is God's only plan for reaching the entire world with the truth of His glory and love. Regardless of what we've made it into, God remains completely committed to His church. So must we.

5.1 CHURCH

No, your eyes aren't deceiving you. The first word in this session on church is just that—*church*. Before we look further at words we overuse in the church, we need to first unpack what we mean when we talk about church. First and foremost we must recognize that we often use the word "church" in a completely incorrect way.

Some people think of church as a quaint wooden structure where people eat covered dish meals with good friends. Others consider it the "third place" in their lives, where they find community, enjoy various activities, and temporarily escape from the struggles of work and home life.[1]

On the other hand, an increasing number of people would equate the church with a stuffy building full of hypocritical people. For many, "church" has become a symbol of outdated thinking and judgmental doctrine. Even many Christians consider church to be a necessary (or more accurately, unnecessary, given church attendance) evil; somewhere they're expected to go but that doesn't have a bearing on their private relationships with God.[2]

What's foundationally wrong with all of these perspectives of church, both the positive and the negative, is that each considers church first and foremost a place, a building where people of faith come together once to a few times a week. But the church isn't somewhere we go; it's something we are. And understanding this distinction is critical to fully embracing our role as part of God's church.

LOVING AND SERVING TOGETHER

The word translated "church" in the New Testament is the Greek word *ekklesia*, which comes from the verb meaning "to call out." Therefore, "church" is the designation of those who have been called out by God. Out of darkness into light. Out of sin into freedom. Out of death into life. The word only refers to a local institution secondarily. Primarily, it denotes a world-wide family of faith that a person becomes a part of when he or she starts walking with Jesus. If you're a Christian, you're part of His church whether you like it or not.

When we look around our world, we see all sorts of things the church should be involved in. Everywhere we turn, we're face-to-face with someone who has needs to be met. Many people look at the description of the very first church, in Acts 2:44-47, as the answer to what the church should be about:

> **"Now all the believers were together and had everything in common. So they sold their possessions and property and distributed the proceeds to all, as anyone had a need. And every day they devoted themselves to meeting**

---

 1. In *Pour Your Heart Into It*, Howard Schultz, Starbucks' CEO, says his company grew because people saw it as a "third place."

 2. How many? Roughly 90 percent of young adults, according to research in the book *Lost and Found*.[vii]

together in the temple complex, and broke bread from house to house. They ate their food with gladness and simplicity of heart, praising God and having favor with all the people. And every day the Lord added to them those who were being saved."

The early church was engaged in the regular practice of meaningful community, generosity, worship, serving others, and sharing the gospel with those around them. Our communities of faith must be involved in similar activities.

Those are all things that the church *does*, but what about what the church *is*? The core truth of its identity? To find that, we have to realize that everything in our lives and on this earth is happening on two different levels of reality at the same time.

THE DISPLAY OF GOD'S GLORY

You may be asking yourself, *What does he mean by the whole "two different levels of reality" thing?* Think about it like this: From God's perspective, every physical element of creation was first a spiritual reality to Him. Long before God made rocks, trees, or humans, the spiritual reality of the universe existed. So when He created physical reality as we know it, He did so with these spiritual realities in mind. Examples are everywhere.

Take marriage, for instance. We know marriage is about companionship, love, and growing families. But marriage has a spiritual foundation. In Ephesians 5, Paul reveals that our marriages are meant to be walking, talking, living, breathing illustrations of Christ's relationship with the church.

Or consider another example—food. We might say that food is tangible. The first things that come to my mind right now are catfish, peanuts, and cucumbers. Beyond specific types, food is about nourishment and good sensations to the taste buds. But Jesus used food as a metaphor for people's spiritual hunger. He fed them real bread, but knew they were hungry for spiritual nourishment, which only He, the "bread of life," could give them.[3]

See it? Everything physical can potentially point us to something spiritual. Is it really too much of a stretch to think that the hard texture of a rock points us to the Rock of Ages? Or that the frame of a door points us to Jesus, who knocks on the "door" of our hearts? I don't think so.

So we come to the church. Paul argues that there's something else going on in the church—something we can't see. Consider Ephesians 3:8-11:

"This grace was given to me—the least of all the saints!—to proclaim to the Gentiles the incalculable riches of the Messiah, and to shed light for all about

 3. See John 6 for a more full explanation of the metaphorical way Jesus viewed food.

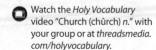 Watch the *Holy Vocabulary* video "Church (chûrch) *n.*" with your group or at *threadsmedia. com/holyvocabulary.*

the administration of the mystery hidden for ages in God who created all things. This is so that God's multi-faceted wisdom may now be made known through the church to the rulers and authorities in the heavens. This is according to the purpose of the ages, which He made in the Messiah, Jesus our Lord."

Pretty amazing stuff, right? Paul claimed that God is using the church to reveal His glorious wisdom and power. And even more amazing is the fact that God isn't just using the church as His revelation on earth; He's also using us to make Himself known to the rulers and authorities in the heavenly realms.

The church has a cosmological, universal purpose that is a bigger extension of its role here on earth. It's as if God has put the church on a shelf in front of the entire universe to be a display of His glory and has said, "Take a look at what things are like when My will is done on earth as it is in heaven." The church is the advance team of the kingdom of God. We could go so far as to say the church is God's Delta Force.

GOD'S ADVANCE TEAM

The Delta Force is an advance team of specially trained agents who act as the precursor for the army.[4] They perform secret missions, do the hard prep work, and engage the enemy before the entire army arrives. They are the ones who announce that the full army is going to invade.

The relationship between the Delta Force and the U.S. Armed Forces is not unlike what Paul described in the Book of Ephesians. In the way that the Delta Force is the advance team for a military invasion, the church and all of her members are the advance team for the coming fullness of God's kingdom. It's God's way of saying, "Look universe! Look where we're headed." The church should be the group of people the world and all of the powers of heaven can look to and see the wisdom, love, power, and glory of God on display. We are the advance team.

The kingdom of God has not yet been fully realized on earth. It will be when Jesus returns.[5] In the meantime, the church is God's showplace, a diverse group of people from around the world, united in our belief in the saving grace of Jesus. We are the evidence of His wisdom. This brings an air of seriousness to things like relationships, caring for needs, worship, and obedience, doesn't it? When we choose to not only *go* to church, but also *be* the church, we take on the task of displaying God's glory to the world. And that's pretty serious business.

---

 4. Chuck Norris starred as Major Scott McCoy in the 1986 movie *The Delta Force*.

 5. Second Thessalonians 1:6-10 describes Jesus' return as a time of reward and judgment, when God's work on earth is finished.

READ. THINK. DISCUSS.

Why do you think people tend to like Jesus but not the church?

How do you think local bodies of believers relate to the church as a whole?

How important is it for you to be involved in a local expression of the church? Why?

What are some ways you might encourage your church to more fully embody its mission as the advance team of the kingdom of God?

5.2 KINGDOM

Although people often refer to the individual "books" of the Bible, the Bible isn't a group of random texts by different writers who composed varying accounts of what happened in "Bible times." Through the guidance and inspiration of the Holy Spirit, the Bible is one, continuous, engaging narrative about God and His work in the universe. And it's a great story when you think about it.

The story is about a mighty King who rules over all the land. Part of His kingdom, though, was subverted by evil. Over time, many of the inhabitants of that land forgot who the rightful King is and no longer cared about His rule. But because of His great love, the King sent ambassadors into the kingdom to reclaim the land and remind the people that He is their King. Time and time again, though, the ambassadors' messages were rejected, until the King finally sent His own Son into the hostile territory.

Though His Son was rejected by many, He began to gather followers together—those who saw the goodness and grace of the true King—and reunite them with their rightful ruler. The movement continued as more and more people, from inside that hostile territory, began to follow the leadership of the Son and the rule of His Father.

That's what the church is—a group of ambassadors living in a foreign land, working to subvert evil and bring about a massive return of God's people to relationships with Him. The church is the living representation of the kingdom of God on earth.

ALREADY, BUT NOT YET

Jesus frequently talked about the kingdom of God.[6] The phrase "kingdom of God" is found in more than 50 separate sayings in the Gospels, many more if you count the portions of those books that overlap.[7] Understanding what the Bible says about God's kingdom is essential to grasping the church's role in the world.

Let's first look at what Scripture says about the timing of the kingdom of God. Is the kingdom here already, or is it something we're waiting on? Jesus' words about the presence of the kingdom of God seem to contradict each other.

For example, passages like Luke 11:2 and Mark 14:25 suggest the kingdom of God is a future reality—something that is to come. But then other passages, such as Luke 11:20 and Luke 17:21, imply that the kingdom of God is here, already at hand.

So the question remains: Is it here or not? The answer is yes . . . and yes. The kingdom of God is *already* here, but *not yet* here.

 6. Eight of Jesus' parables are about the kingdom of God. They're found in Matthew 13 and Mark 4:26-29.

 7. The *Synopsis of the Four Gospels* is a useful tool to help you study the Gospels side by side.

In his book *Sent: Living the Missional Nature of the Church*, Ed Stetzer includes the following illustration of the "already, but not yet" state of the church:

> "Think of it like this: At the end of World War II, there were two important historical dates. The first date is remembered as D-Day—June 6, 1944. The Allied Powers effectively broke the back of the Axis Powers when they stormed the beach at Normandy. By taking that beach, they secured the victory, and it was just a matter of time until the war was over. However, the official war continued on until May 7-8, 1945, when the Allied Powers accepted the unconditional and full surrender of Germany. Then the fighting stopped completely.
>
> Almost a full year of fighting, shooting, and casualties took place between the time when the victory was secured and when the victory was declared. Though the outcome was sure, there were still battles to be fought in the meantime."[8]

We are living in a similar "meantime" state, in the midst of the battle between God and evil. The kingdom of God burst into the world with the birth of Jesus Christ. He came in God's power to redeem God's creation, and His resurrection from the dead secured victory over sin and death. The end is no longer in doubt. God wins. But there are still smaller battles to be fought. There is still a kingdom to be advanced, and we must do our part to advance it until the day when Jesus splits the sky and comes back again, ending our battle with evil and completing God's redemption of the world.[9] Until that day, the kingdom will remain "already here," but "not yet" fully present.

ON EARTH AS IT IS IN HEAVEN

In this meantime, the church is the representative of the kingdom of God on earth. That means that the values, priorities, and goal of the kingdom should be fully represented in the church. When people look at the church, they should have a visual representation of what the kingdom of God will be like when Jesus returns.

We just looked at what Scripture has to say about the timing of God's kingdom. So what do we learn from Scripture about the kingdom's spiritual and physical nature? Jesus said in Luke 17:21:

"The kingdom of God is among you."

And it is. The kingdom is both a physical and spiritual reality. It's the realm in which God's reign is fully realized. Spiritually, this means that the kingdom is where we live by faith in Christ and fully give ourselves to the purposes of God. Physically, it's where there is an effort to bring about justice, comfort, and provision.

---

8. Ed Stetzer, *Sent: Living the Missional Nature of the Church* (Nashville: LifeWay Press, 2008), 36.

9. In his letter to Titus, Paul described Jesus' second coming as the "blessed hope" of the church (Titus 2:13).

The church must work to bring about both of these realities on earth. We share the good news of salvation in Christ, and we feed the hungry. We talk about growing in intimacy with God, and we give shelter to the homeless. Living out the kingdom isn't an either/or, but a both/and. Through the church as the representative of God's kingdom, justice is done. People are cared for. The lost are welcomed.

KINGDOM UNITY

The church should embody another characteristic of the kingdom of God as well. The kingdom of God knows no discrimination based on race, culture, or socioeconomic status. God's kingdom has no walls, therefore God's church must not have walls either.

One of the principles of church growth involves creating homogeneous groups. It is commonly practiced that the most effective way of growing a church is to create a group where people look, dress, earn, and act similarly to each other. The idea behind such a design is that people feel most comfortable and attracted to groups of people who are like them. By forming churches in this manner, we can target a specific group of people, gear all our marketing efforts toward them, and hope to create a buzz within that specific group. The homogeneous unit that's created becomes the core of the church. And this model works. Make no mistake, it works. Well. But just because it works doesn't mean it's what God intended.

In truth, I like being in churches where people look like me. I know they're thinking what I'm thinking. They're feeling similar things to what I'm feeling. It's comfortable there. And all of that makes church easier. Only one problem—that's not what heaven is going to be like.

If the church is the representation of the kingdom of God, then we should model the look of our churches after what the kingdom of God is like. When we look at Scripture, we see that God has always been cultivating a people of His own, and that people represents every tribe, tongue, and nation on earth. In heaven, everyone will retain their cultural identities. We'll hear every language being spoken before the throne of Jesus in one muddled but beautiful roar:

> **"After this I looked, and there was a vast multitude from every nation, tribe, people, and language, which no one could number, standing before the throne and before the Lamb. They were robed in white with palm branches in their hands. And they cried out in a loud voice: Salvation belongs to our God, who is seated on the throne, and to the Lamb!" (Revelation 7:9-10).**

The church of today is supposed to be a glimpse into the future. It's a foretaste, a preview of what eternity will be like. How, then, can we allow ourselves to cultivate a church experience where we all look the same? To do so denies the purposes of God in His kingdom.

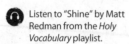 Listen to "Shine" by Matt Redman from the *Holy Vocabulary* playlist.

READ. THINK. DISCUSS.

If someone asked you what the kingdom of God is, what would you say?

What is the church's relationship to the kingdom of God?

Which do you gravitate more toward—seeing the kingdom as a spiritual reality or a physical one? Why is that not an either/or kind of choice?

How diverse are your relationships? Why does it matter to God that you are in community with people who are different than you are?

What are some ways you might help your church more fully embody the kingdom of God?

5.3 ORDINANCES

OK—I admit it. *Ordinances* isn't necessarily an over-churched term. In fact, you might be pinching your eyebrows together trying to remember exactly what an ordinance is. And that's part of the problem—it depends on who you ask. It seems that virtually every denomination has its own take on the nature of the ordinances, what they do or do not symbolize, how they're practiced, and even how many there are. So even though you might not use the word regularly, chances are you've had an experience involving these signs of the Christian faith if you've hung around church for a while.

While the contemporary Christian subculture might lead us to think that having fish stickers on our car bumpers or crosses on our T-shirts are signs of our faith, the practice of ordinances actually carry deep meaning. (And they're way older.) They're the lasting declarations of the faith, passed down from Jesus Himself through the early church; believers' actions that have withstood the test of 2,000 years, and today still serve as the marks and consistent practices of those who are part of the church of Jesus Christ.

BAPTISM AND THE LORD'S SUPPER

In Protestant churches, there are only two recognized ordinances—baptism and the Lord's Supper (aka Communion). Much ink has been spilled over both the "sign" part and the "mystery" part of these ordinances. Most traditions tend to lean to one direction or the other. Either they look at baptism and the Lord's Supper exclusively as signs, or they look at them exclusively as mysterious, spiritual events.

For those who interpret the ordinances as signs, the typical belief is that baptism and the Lord's Supper are outward symbols of how a person's inner self has changed through belief in Jesus. In the case of baptism, a person being submerged in water is symbolic of Jesus' death, burial, and resurrection. Paul put it like this in Romans 6:4-5:

> **"Therefore we were buried with Him by baptism into death, in order that, just as Christ was raised from the dead by the glory of the Father, so we too may walk in a new way of life. For if we have been joined with Him in the likeness of His death, we will certainly also be in the likeness of His resurrection."**

When Christ died, so did all who believe in Him. And if we are united with His death, we are also united with His resurrection. Baptism is a symbolic reminder of that union and the new life we enter into in Christ. Likewise, the Lord's Supper is a sign of our relationship with Jesus. Jesus Himself, in talking about the Lord's Supper, said that we should do it "in remembrance of Me," and that by eating the bread and drinking the cup we proclaim His death visibly until He returns (1 Corinthians 11:23-25).

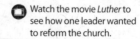 Watch the movie *Luther* to see how one leader wanted to reform the church.

Those who lean in the direction of mystery might agree with some of the symbolism of these acts, but they see the ordinances as being far more powerful. To them, calling these rites nothing more than "symbols" diminishes their significance in the life of the church. They believe baptism isn't symbolic, but a requirement for salvation. This opinion takes very literally Peter's statement that people should be baptized for the forgiveness of sins (Acts 2:38), to the point of saying that without baptism a person can't be truly forgiven.

People who hold this opinion might also take the words of Jesus in Matthew 26 very literally. When He said, "This is My body," and, "This is My blood," they believe He wasn't being metaphorical. According to some traditions, the elements of the Lord's Supper literally transform into the body and blood of Christ during the ritual.[10]

VISIBLE REMINDERS OF INVISIBLE REALITIES

When we consider what Scripture reveals about the ordinances, we have to acknowledge their symbolic nature. Baptism is a symbol of the internal union with Christ;[11] the bread and the cup are symbolic of Jesus' body and blood shed on our behalf.[12] And yet the problem with that interpretation is the tendency to treat these ordinances as "just symbols." Doing so enables us to approach them casually, sometimes forgetting the reverence and awe they deserve.

My son Joshua is 5 years old. As a 5-year-old, he now gets to come to "big church," and I'll be honest—it's a struggle for all of us. He's just learning to read, so most of the songs go a little too fast for him to keep up with the words. The sermon is the only time during the week when Joshua has to sit still in one place and listen for 45 minutes. So we usually come to church armed with coloring books, crayons, and a whole lot of patience.

The biggest struggle, though, is Lord's Supper day. When we walk into church and see the cloth-covered table at the front of the auditorium, I can't help but steel my nerves for the inevitable confrontation that's coming. I know that Joshua is going to be upset.

Is Joshua going to be upset because he wants to remember the sacrifice of Jesus on his behalf? Because he wants to appreciate that Christ bore the wrath of God so that he might be free from sin and death? Nope—he's upset because he wants a snack. And every time those little cups of juice and the plate of tiny wafers pass him by, he begins to think of it like the forbidden fruit in Eden.

That's not so different from the way we might look at the Lord's Supper, or at least be tempted to look at it. Yes, it's symbolic in nature, but we've got to fight the impulse to simply scarf down a little cracker and chase it with some juice. Perhaps we need to add a little more mystery into our understanding.

---

 10. Some say the phrase "hocus pocus" comes from the Latin used at the moment when the elements supposedly change.

 11. Read Matthew 28:19; Acts 10:47-48; Acts 16:32-33; and Acts 18:7-8.

 12. Check out Luke 22:19-20 and 1 Corinthians 11:26.

The Bible affirms the symbolic aspect of baptism and the Lord's Supper, but we can't deny the element of mystery associated with these acts. Consider, for example, the sobering words of Paul in 1 Corinthians 11:30:

"This is why many are sick and ill among you, and many have fallen asleep."

"Fallen asleep" is the polite way to say "died." Evidently there were some people not taking the Lord's Supper seriously enough, and their casual approach to the ordinance had serious, even deadly, consequences.

We would do well to make sure our belief in the symbolism of the ordinances doesn't lead us into the casual and haphazard observance of these acts. They deserve our full belief and reverence, for they are visible reminders of invisible realities. These ordinances are the means Jesus left for us to remind ourselves of the spiritual realities at work in our lives. We might say that baptism and the Lord's Supper are aids to help our senses catch up to our faith.[13]

THE COMMON BECOMES UNCOMMON

If the ordinances are symbolic of some of the most profound realities of our relationship with God, then we need to consider another question: Why such common elements? I mean, the ordinances focus on water, bread, and wine, three quite common things.[14]

If these are the two tangible ways Jesus left for the church to commemorate, appreciate, and testify to the invisible realities of salvation, we might wonder why He didn't chose something more special. Shouldn't we be taking the Lord's Supper with caviar? Shouldn't baptism be done in the world's most purified water? Tap water and bread feel too unimportant.

Perhaps the elements themselves are meant to be symbolic too, reminding us of another spiritual reality. If we look at the life of the Son of God, we notice it is strikingly common. Jesus never lived extravagantly; He took the common things of the world around Him and made them holy. Everything from a birthplace to a wedding, a woman, a tree, or a fish had greater value after being influenced by Christ.

The greatest example of Jesus making the common uncommon is us. Me and you. Who are we that we should be called sons or daughters of the God of the universe? We were His enemies, common, everyday rebels, but when His Son entered into our lives, we became very uncommon. We became extraordinary.

Brother Lawrence wrote many years ago in *The Practice of the Presence of God* that to him, washing pots and pans all day long in a monastery was a holy act.[15] Not because of the job

---

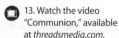 13. Watch the video "Communion," available at *threadsmedia.com*.

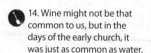 14. Wine might not be that common to us, but in the days of the early church, it was just as common as water.

15. Brother Lawrence, *The Practice of the Presence of God* (Grand Rapids: Spire Books, 2006), 11-14.

itself, but because he did so with a sense of the closeness of Jesus. And where Jesus is, the common becomes uncommon. Such is the case with His church.

Perhaps we are meant to celebrate the common becoming uncommon with ordinary things. That's what we do with these ordinances. That's why even though they're symbolic, they're also mysterious. They're common, but then again, they're so much more.

READ. THINK. DISCUSS.

When was the last time you took the Lord's Supper or experienced a baptism service? What was your attitude?

Why do you think Jesus chose baptism and the Lord's Supper as symbols of our union with Him and His sacrifice for us, respectively?

Why is it helpful to have these tangible reminders of spiritual realities?

What might need to change in the way you approach baptism and the Lord's Supper?

Take the opportunity to share the story of your baptism with someone.

5.4 BODY

The church has a lot of adjectives applied to it these days, and not all are positive: stuffy, outdated, anti-cultural, backward, misguided, hypocritical. And the list could go on. Surely that's a far cry from the biblical description of this group of called-out followers of Jesus. If we look to the pages of Scripture, we find helpful descriptions of exactly who and what the church is meant to be.

One of the most prominent words used by New Testament writers to describe the church is "body." There it is pictured as the body of Christ. The apostle Paul seems to be especially fond of this metaphor, considering he writes about the church as the body of Christ in Romans, 1 Corinthians, Ephesians, and Colossians.

It seems pretty important, then, for us to dig a little deeper into the this word if we want to examine the nature of the church. Perhaps, though, we should start by realizing that this language isn't strictly metaphorical. We, as the church, literally are the physical representation of Christ in the world. Paul wrote, regarding the position of Jesus as the King of the universe:

> **"And He [God] put everything under His [Jesus'] feet and appointed Him as head over everything for the church, which is His body, the fullness of the One who fills all things in every way" (Ephesians 1:22-23).**

When Jesus died, He broke down every imaginable barrier between us and God. That's why the curtain in the temple that separated the holy of holies from the outside was ripped down the middle.[16] Through Jesus, we have access to God. But His death also removed the horizontal barriers between people everywhere. Before Christ, we were all Jews or Gentiles, rich or poor, educated or uneducated, slave or free. But after His death and resurrection, we are all one, united as His followers.[17]

This united group is made up of one type of person—Christians. Not Hispanics. Or Anglos. Or Africans. Or the rich. Christians. That's the church, one in Christ, with each person having the Holy Spirit of Christ dwelling inside him or her. Because of the Holy Spirit in us, the church functions as the body of Christ in the world (Ephesians 2:11-22).

MANY PARTS, ONE BODY

A couple of important principles about the nature of the church surface when we focus on the passages of Scripture that use the "body" description—unity and diversity. Paul expanded on these principles in Romans 12 and 1 Corinthians 12. In both places he wrote at length about what it means to be the body of Christ and how unity and diversity play equally critical roles.

---

 16. The curtain was ripped from top to bottom. Another reminder that the breaking down of walls was from God, not humanity.

 17. "There is no Jew or Greek, slave or free, male or female; for you are all one in Christ Jesus" (Galatians 3:28).

We know the devastating effects of a part of our bodies going rogue—cancer develops. That's when a particular cell, though seemingly small, decides for whatever reason to stop doing what it was created to do. It changes its objective, and pretty soon disease spreads throughout the entire system. All from a single, tiny, minuscule cell.

The body only functions correctly when every part is working in unity toward the same goal. When the legs, arms, heart, blood vessels, eyes, and all the other members of the body are functioning in accordance with their given roles, the body is able to operate appropriately and effectively.

Much in the same way, the church must be unified in order for it to accomplish its mission on earth. As Paul noted,

> **"Now as we have many parts in one body, and all the parts do not have the same function, in the same way we who are many are one body in Christ and individually members of one another" (Romans 12:4-5).**

Unity is so important to the body of Christ that it was one of the main themes of Jesus' great prayer for His future followers in John 17. He prayed like this:

> **"May they all be one, as You, Father, are in Me and I am in You. May they also be one in Us, so the world may believe You sent me" (John 17:21).**

The need for unity makes sense when you think about it. The church is presenting a way of living that is radically counter-cultural.

In his famous "Letter from Birmingham Jail," Martin Luther King Jr. shared his frustration with the church's failure to live up to its identity as the counter-cultural, unified body of Christ during the civil rights movement:

> "In deep disappointment I have wept over the laxity of the church. But be assured that my tears have been tears of love. There can be no deep disappointment where there is not deep love. Yes, I love the church. How could I do otherwise? I am in the rather unique position of being the son, the grandson and the great-grandson of preachers. Yes, I see the church as the body of Christ. But, oh! How we have blemished and scarred that body through social neglect and through fear of being nonconformists."[18]

We talk and preach about the fundamental issues of right and wrong, good and evil, truth and falsehood. And we claim that people's eternal destinies hang in the balance. What reason would any level-headed person have to listen to that message if the people

---

18. Martin Luther King Jr., "Letter from Birmingham Jail" [online], April 16, 1963 [cited May 6, 2010]. Available from the Internet: *mlk-kpp01.stanford.edu*.

proclaiming it can't even agree on what color carpet to have in their buildings? Unity is absolutely essential in the body of Christ. Even a little cancer is too much because it never stays little for long. It eventually spreads.

Let's be careful, however, to not mistake unity for uniformity. In as much as Paul was concerned with unity, he was concerned that the unity was achieved through diversity. In his own words,

> **"For as the body is one and has many parts, and all the parts of that body, though many, are one body—so also is Christ. For we were all baptized by one Spirit into one body—whether Jews or Greeks, whether slaves or free—and we were all made to drink of one Spirit" (1 Corinthians 12:12-13).**

For the body to function properly, each part must be convinced of its own role. The eyes are meant to see. The legs are meant to walk. The heart is meant to pump blood. It's laughable to think about the hands trying to hear or the feet trying to smell, and yet that's exactly the problem in many of our churches.

The body of Christ has work to do in the world, and we've got too many mouths. Or at least too many people who think they're mouths. We don't have enough hands or hearts to accomplish our tasks. The body only works when the diversity of its parts is fully embraced and given whole-heartedly to the bigger goal at hand—spreading the gospel.

EVERY PART IS VITAL

In order for a church to function as a healthy body, we must first convince one another that we are critical parts of the body. Somehow we've become convinced that only a select few are equipped to really "serve the Lord." Typically, these are preachers, worship leaders, missionaries, or Sunday School teachers; the rest of us are just regular people.

That attitude reveals that down deep inside of us we believe there is an invisible line between the secular and the sacred. We think some moments of our lives are reserved for the sacred, like those moments when we go to the church building, but the majority of our days are spent engaging in regular secular moments. Like walking the dog or going to work. But the truth is there's no such line.[19]

Consequently, everyone is a minister of Jesus Christ, and we don't have an off switch. The church is primarily made up of Christians, whose secondary roles may be teachers, or bankers, or chefs. First and foremost, we are followers of Christ, and every single one of us is vital.

....

 19. "We do religion with our hearts and minds, but we also do religion with our bodies." –Lauren Winner[viii]

Take away a limb from the body, and the body might adapt. But it will do so with great difficulty. Even then, it's certainly not functioning perfectly. Likewise, in the body of Christ, there is no room for pride in one's supposed position. We all must recognize the essential diversity within the body and appreciate each member for what he or she uniquely brings to the church.

That's the body of Christ—unity in diversity, all functioning together for the common goal of being Jesus' hands and feet in the world.

READ. THINK. DISCUSS.

Which part of the body are you? Why?

What about this "body" language is helpful to your understanding of the church?

Can you think of some of the other ways the church is described in Scripture? Which of those descriptions are meaningful to you? Why?

Do you see the line between the secular and the sacred in your own life? What can you do to get rid of it?

5.5 MISSION

People who have been called out. That's a very basic definition for the Greek word *ekklesia*, which is translated into English as "church." We have been called, as the children of God, from darkness into light. From evil into good. From life without God to eternity with Him. But what's our mission, our purpose for being called out?

If we look at the trend of churches over the last 25 years or so, we might answer that question in a number of ways. It may appear as if the church has been called out to build buildings, start programs, and educate its members. All of those elements have one thing in common: They are about the internal functions of the church and its members.

The problem is that the church hasn't been called out for its own purpose, but for the sake of the world around it. We've been blessed in order to be a blessing to others. That is the foundation of the church—a people on mission together, moving out into the world.[20]

OUTWARD FOCUSED LIVES

In Matthew 16, Peter made a dramatic confession of Jesus:

> "'You are the Messiah, the Son of the living God!' And Jesus responded, 'Simon son of Jonah, you are blessed because flesh and blood did not reveal this to you, but My Father in heaven. And I also say to you that you are Peter, and on this rock I will build My church, and the forces of Hades will not overpower it. I will give you the keys of the kingdom of heaven, and whatever you bind on earth is already bound in heaven, and whatever you loose on earth is already loosed in heaven'" (Matthew 16:16-19).

Without going into too much detail about this passage, the language is striking.[21] While it's true that the bit about hell not overtaking the church seems defensive in nature, the fact that the church is binding and loosing and attacking the forces of darkness proves we, as called-out people, are meant to be on the move. We are the ground troops of the kingdom of God, reuniting lost people with their King.

The offensive, forward march of the church is reiterated in verses like John 20:21:

> "As the Father has sent Me, I also send you."

You can say a lot of things about God. You can say that He's holy, loving, glorious, and just. But you also have to acknowledge that God is a sender. Just as He sent Jesus, Jesus sent out the church. Explicitly, we see Jesus' sending in the Great Commission and its reiteration in Acts 1:8:

---

 20. "Mission is understanding the intention of God and then acting on it." –Ed Stetzer[ix]

 21. The Roman Catholic tradition claims this passage establishes Peter as the first pope. Others argue that the rock upon which the church is built is Peter's confession of Jesus Christ as Lord.

> "But you will receive power when the Holy Spirit has come upon you, and you will be My witnesses in Jerusalem, in all Judea and Samaria, and to the ends of the earth."

Here's the thing, though—God didn't wake up one morning and decide to start sending people out. He's been doing it for a long, long time. The first missionary wasn't Peter. Or Paul. Or even Jesus. We find hints of the Great Commission in the Book of Genesis.

Remember Abram, who would later become Abraham? It's interesting to see how similar God's charge to him was to what we find at the end of the Gospels and in the Book of Acts:

> "The LORD said to Abram: 'Go out from your land, your relatives, and your father's house to the land that I will show you. I will make you into a great nation, I will bless you, I will make your name great, and you will be a blessing. I will bless those who bless you, I will curse those who treat you with contempt, and all the peoples on earth will be blessed through you'" (Genesis 12:1-3).

Very, very similar, right? Thousands of years ago, God commissioned Abram and his descendants to spread throughout the whole world and become a blessing to all the peoples of the earth. How were they to be that blessing? They would bless the world by taking their knowledge and experience of God with them, introducing people from every tribe, tongue, nation, and people to this God.

Abraham and his kids were sent out to be witnesses. Mission-oriented witnesses. And the church is the New Testament incarnation of God's promise and commission of Abraham.

The church, regardless of the specifics of musical taste, approach to evangelism, or treatment of spiritual gifts, is sent by God to do His work. We're people on mission, thrust into the world by Jesus. Unfortunately, though, the church seems to have lost its offensive nature.

Rather than obeying the call to go out into the world, the church seems to have retreated inside its walls, preferring a defensive posture rather than an offensive one. Think of it as the equivalent of Abram saying, "Nice idea, God, but I think I'm going to stay right here in my own country. I can build a good-looking city here, complete with big walls to keep all the 'bad people' out."

Regardless of the best intentions of buildings, programs, and Christian education, those efforts reflect a "come to us" mentality. Indeed, many church bodies have taught for a long time that the job of their members is to get as many people as possible inside their walls.

We have programs "in here." We talk about God "in here." We proclaim the gospel "in here." And "in here" we try to model the kingdom of God. I suppose that's not necessarily a bad thing, but slowly the focus has drifted further and further in. Churches now are in large part efforts at insulating members from the surrounding culture, and church members tiptoe through their lives making sure no sin gets on their shoes.

While it's true that Christians—and by proxy the church—are to keep themselves from being negatively influenced by the world, they aren't to do so apart from living in the world. In fact, Jesus made a point to pray in John 17 that God would not take His followers from the world:

> "I am not praying that You take them out of the world but that You protect them from the evil one. They are not of the world, as I am not of the world. Sanctify them by the truth; Your word is truth. As you sent Me into the world, I also have sent them into the world" (John 17:15-18).

Our efforts at secluding ourselves, then, contradict this priestly prayer of Jesus on our behalf.

No, the church isn't supposed to have an "in here" mentality. It's supposed to have an "out there" mentality. The "out there" is emphasized in the Great Commission in Matthew 28:19,

> "Go, therefore, and make disciples of all nations . . ."

The verb *go* is an imperative one; it's a command. But it's also a continuous action. The sense is "as you are going." That means that the church is meant to be in a constant state of motion, always moving out into the world. Always taking new territory for the kingdom. Always pushing the boundaries to introduce more people to God.

A TESTIMONY TO THE NATIONS

The imperative command of the mission is in the DNA of the church, whether we recognize it or not. It's who we are as the people of God. He has not called us out in order to build mini-kingdoms; He's called us out to expand His. This calling isn't limited to people we refer to as "vocational missionaries." Their call is unique as is any career calling.[22] The church's call to be on mission for God is universal, so you and I have no excuse.

Notice the same emphasis Jesus had in the Sermon on the Mount. The people of God are called two things in that passage: salt and light. Though both of those elements have different purposes, what they have in common is that they are utterly pointless unless they are implemented in their mission. Whether adding light to the cultural pathway of the world or bringing taste to an otherwise dull existence, the church is meant to be working in the world.

22. Ruth A. Tucker's *From Jerusalem to Irian Jaya* tells the stories of hundreds who fulfilled calls to full-time missions.

This is the mission of the church, and it's a mission that must be accomplished. Jesus has thrown all His weight behind the church accomplishing this mission to the exclusion of every other organization. Social programs, humanitarian aid, and rock stars might have the best of intentions and do much good, but the only thing in the universe Jesus has endorsed for His mission is the church. There is no plan B.

Until the church embraces its mission fully and completely, we'll always be living in a sort of limbo. Indeed, the return of Jesus has been linked to the accomplishment of the church's work:

> "This good news of the kingdom will be proclaimed in all the world as a testimony to all nations. And then the end will come" (Matthew 24:14).

That puts the goals of our churches into sharp focus. We may build buildings, have programs, and encourage membership, but in the end, the church is on earth for one thing and one thing only: to extend the message of Jesus to the farthest corners of the world. That mission must drive our budgets, our programs, and our thinking. It must be priority one, in such a way that everything else the church does should be measured against it.

READ. THINK. DISCUSS.

Do you contribute to an "in here" mentality or an "out there" mentality in your church?

Which is easier for you? Why?

Why do you think churches tend to turn inward on themselves?

How can you contribute to an "out there" mentality for your own church?

Leading a group? It's the way to go. Find discussion questions and teaching tools in the leader kit, available on *threadsmedia.com/holyvocabulary*.

END TIMES

AWAITING THE END TIMES

Ah, the images of Revelation. Extreme pictures of everything from God's judgment to the throne of His glory come to mind when we consider the end of time (or eschatology, to use the "church" word). It's ironic how much of Christianity is about looking forward to eternity and yet how little about the future we really understand. Anyone who has spent time reading the Book of Revelation has most likely come away at least a little bit disturbed and probably a lot confused. In fact, one might wonder why this book of confusing images and strange details is in the Bible to begin with.

Revelation wasn't written to cause controversy. Nor was it written to inspire fear. Revelation is included in the Bible for the expressed purpose of instilling hope in the believing community.

God makes many promises about eternity. The Bible talks extensively about faith in things to come, the glory of heaven, and the torments of hell. What God doesn't promise, however, is a life of ease and comfort in the here and now. Far from it, in fact. But that's where those images and promises of the end times come into play.

We are meant to love the last things, because they are the consummation of our faith. At the end, faith will be irrelevant. We won't have to *believe* any more, for belief will be replaced by sight. The intangible presence of God will become tangible. The distant future will become the eternal present. And embracing the reality of the last things—however surreal they may seem to us—means great change in the here and now.

We know the end of the story.

Oh, we might not know specifics, like the identity of the Antichrist or the exact day of Jesus' return, but we do know this: Good, and God, wins.

Because we know the end of the story, we can survive in the present. We can live confidently amid the suffering and trials of our world, because we've already read the conclusion. That's what fuels our hope right now—not what might be, but what will surely be. Forever.

6.1 JUDGMENT

Besides watching college football, one of my other favorite pastimes is judging others. Unlike the football watching, I can do this all year long. Chances are, if our paths have ever crossed, I've judged you for one thing or another. Could've been for anything, like how much TV you watch. Or what kind of car you drive. Or the way you eat your soup. And I'm not alone in my passion for judgment.

One of the most quoted verses in the Bible is Matthew 7:1:

> **"Do not judge, so that you won't be judged."**

This verse is quoted by Christians and non-Christians alike. Don't be too quick to pat the world on the back for its biblical knowledge, though. I'm not convinced we use this verse in the way Jesus intended it when He said it. When we quote this verse, we do so with the intent to self-justify. We want to validate our own behavior, so we try to enlist Jesus in our cause: "Who are you to judge me? I can rob all the gas stations I want to! Remember what Jesus said . . ." Something tells me that's not what the Son of God meant when He included this short command as part of a lengthy teaching series on how to pursue godly living in a very ungodly world.[1]

Our judgment of others is rooted in comparisons and insecurities. We may look at someone and think badly of them because of how they spend their money or time. But usually we have those thoughts because we're insecure about how we're spending our own. It makes us feel better to know that at least we're not as bad as someone else.

In the Matthew 7 passage, Jesus wasn't saying that we have to stand idly by and watch wrong being done. He was, though, reminding us that judging the deeds of others isn't our responsibility. It's God's.

SHEEP, GOATS, AND GOD'S JUDGMENT

As uncomfortable as the thought may be, we can't really think about the end times without thinking about God's judgment. When Jesus returns and the world as we know it is brought to an end, every human being who has ever walked the face of the earth will stand before the judgment seat of Christ.[2] At that time, God's perfect justice will be vindicated.

So what are Christians to think about this inevitability? We are counting on the fact that Jesus is our propitiation, that God chose to punish Him instead of us.[3] Will judgment day for all the Christians simply result in getting a pass through the pearly gates? The Bible suggests there will be more to it than that.

---

 1. Jesus preached the Sermon on the Mount to His disciples, but like always, His teaching attracted a large crowd.

 2. See Romans 14:10, 2 Corinthians 5:10, and Hebrews 4:13 for a few verses on this topic.

 3. Look back at pages 70-73 for a review of what it means that Jesus is our "propitiation."

Take, for example, the various passages of Scripture that state God's judgment will be doled out according to what men and women have done.[4] Nowhere is it recorded in a more sobering fashion than Romans 2:6-8:

> **"He will repay each one according to his works: eternal life to those who by patiently doing good seek for glory, honor, and immortality; but wrath and indignation to those who are self-seeking and disobey the truth, but are obeying unrighteousness."**[5]

See the problem? We've built our entire eternal security on what we believe, often to the detriment of what we do. We are saved by grace, not by works, and this is what we tell ourselves over and over again. How do we reconcile that with these verses that clearly state our works matter?

Getting our heads around how God will judge us is further complicated when we read Jesus' teachings about judgment. Take, for example, the story of the sheep and the goats found in Matthew 25. It begins like this:

> **"When the Son of Man comes in His glory, and all the angels with Him, then He will sit on the throne of His glory. All the nations will be gathered before Him, and He will separate them one from another, just as a shepherd separates the sheep from the goats. He will put the sheep on His right and the goats on the left" (Matthew 25:31-33).**

Fairly straightforward thus far—some people are represented by sheep and others by goats. But things get a little more sticky as we read on. When Jesus gave the reasons for separating one from the other, He listed the good works of the sheep and the lack of good works of the goats. The sheep fed the hungry. They gave the thirsty a cup of cold water. They opened up their homes and practiced hospitality. And the list goes on.

The goats, on the other hand, did none of these things for the least of humanity, and therefore they didn't do them for Jesus. The result is good news for the sheep; very, very bad news for the goats.

This parable should stir up many things in our hearts. It ought to make us question the way we spend our time and energy. It should make us consider our priorities and attitudes. And it threatens to make us reconsider whether or not a person is saved by faith from God's wrath.

To really understand what this story tells us about God's future judgment, though, we must look at a crucial detail: the timing of how everything in the story unfolds. Jesus' illustration

 4. There are many. Matthew 16:27, 2 Corinthians 5:10, and Revelation 22:12 will get you started.

 5. In Romans 2:6 Paul quotes both Psalm 62:12 and Proverbs 24:12.

doesn't depict a cosmic trial each person must attend after he or she dies. No one steps up to the witness stand, delivers a presentation of his or her life's works, and waits for God to make the sheep or goat declaration. No, in Jesus' story the people were called sheep or goats first, and then they were divided, according to their identity. Sheep went with the sheep. Goats went with the goats. Then, after that division, we learned the ramifications of that identity.

CHANGED TO THE CORE

How Jesus judged the nations was completely contingent on who they were at the core of their beings. It's not unlike what James, the brother of Jesus, taught in His letter:

> "What good is it, my brothers, if someone says he has faith, but does not have works? Can his faith save him? If a brother or sister is without clothes and lacks daily food, and one of you says to them, 'Go in peace, keep warm, and eat well,' but you don't give them what the body needs, what good is it? In the same way faith, if it doesn't have works, is dead by itself" (James 2:14-17).

Faith always leads to works. Always. Without exception. Genuine faith in Jesus is changing faith. It is belief that works itself into every crevice of life. Christians are changed people. And their new value system reflects their Savior's. They love what He loves. They do what He does. They follow Him where He goes. And by doing so, they prove the authenticity of their supposed conversion. The authenticity of those described as sheep is evident in how they responded to Jesus. Look back at Matthew 25:37-39:

> "Then the righteous will answer Him, 'Lord, when did we see You hungry and feed You, or thirsty and give You something to drink? When did we see You a stranger and take You in, or without clothes and clothe You? When did we see You sick, or in prison, and visit You?'"

It's as if the sheep stared at each other with confusion. Then collectively, with much clearing of throats and maybe a little stuttering, they looked up at the King of the universe and said, "Umm . . . are You sure we did those things?" They didn't remember doing all that good stuff because it was so natural for them. It was simply the way they lived their lives. Those actions of helping and comforting and visiting and feeding were so intertwined with their lives that they became ordinary. Never once did they do them and think, *Boy, now God is going to let me into heaven.* They just did them, because those works were an expression of who they were.

Far from teaching a works-based salvation, this parable about God's judgment actually confirms the great truth of the gospel—the inner make-up of who we are is completely changed by faith in Jesus. And the truest expression of who we are is to do good.

 Watch the *Holy Vocabulary* video "End Times (ĕnd tīmz) *n.*" with your group or at *threadsmedia.com/holyvocabulary.*

MOTIVATION IS EVERYTHING

Separating the "sheep" from the "goats" isn't the only noteworthy aspect of God's judgment. There's another passage we ought to pay quite a bit of attention to. This one comes from Paul:

> "If anyone builds on the foundation with gold, silver, costly stones, wood, hay, or straw, each one's work will become obvious, for the day will disclose it, because it will be revealed by fire; the fire will test the quality of each one's work. If anyone's work that he has built survives, he will receive a reward. If anyone's work is burned up, it will be lost, but he will be saved; yet it will be like an escape through fire" (1 Corinthians 3:12-15).

Paul made that statement while he was arguing that it really didn't matter who was winning the apostle popularity contest. Some people liked Apollos best. Some people liked Paul. It didn't matter, because in judgment, those who build on the foundation of Jesus Christ will have their work tested, too. On judgment day, we'll see what our good works are really made of. Are they made of selfish ambition? Are they continued efforts to earn the salvation we already have? Are they an attempt to show off and build ourselves up? If so, they'll be swept away.

But if we choose now to build on the foundation of salvation with good—real good, done wholeheartedly out of love for Jesus—then that will be revealed, too. Judgment is indeed coming. Could be tomorrow. Let's make sure we're sheep. And then let's make sure we're building with the right materials.

READ. THINK. DISCUSS.

What's your attitude when thinking about the judgment of God? Apathy? Fear? Confidence?

What do you think the attitude of the Christian ought to be?

How does having a proper understanding of judgment influence the way you live in the present?

How do the passages from Matthew 25 and 1 Corinthians 3 fit together in your mind?

6.2 ETERNITY

If we think of time like a line, which is what we normally do, it just means that the line extends to the right indefinitely. There isn't a point at the end of the line;[6] there is instead an arrow. This is where we begin when we think about eternity—an infinite, timeless state. So when we talk about the eternality of God, we mean that there is never going to be a point when He is not. Forever and ever, God will be.

On more than one occasion, Scripture affirms that one of the blessings of believing in Jesus is the chance to spend eternity in His presence:

> **"For God loved the world in this way: He gave His One and Only Son, so that everyone who believes in Him will not perish but have eternal life" (John 3:16).**

> **"I am the resurrection and the life. The one who believes in Me, even if he dies, will live. Everyone who lives and believes in Me will never die—ever" (John 11:25-26).**

Eternity is a mind-boggling concept, because everything else in our lives has an ending point: second grade, baseball season, engagement, even physical life itself. It's hard enough to wrap our minds around the possibility of existing forever. But what will really mess with our brains isn't that God will always be, or that as Christians we'll always be with Him; it's that God has always *been*. It's one thing to say God has no ending, but to say He has no beginning? That's a little more than my mind can handle.

When we think of eternity, we think of forever. But our concept of forever usually only extends in one direction—to the future. But forever, at least in terms of eternity, must go backward as well. There will never be a point when God is not; and there has never been a point when He was not. He is forever in both directions; that's eternity.

Well, sort of.

In that definition of eternity, we reveal our limited understanding of time. As I've said, we typically think about time linearly. And if we do that, then a line must extend forever in both directions to depict eternity. Living eternally is simply living day after day and year after year in that linear fashion. If we think of God's existence within our limited understanding of time, we automatically assume God is bound by time. But that's simply not true.

God created everything out of nothing, including time. Long before time existed, God existed. In order for God to have invented time, He must exist outside its boundaries. If that's true, then eternity is much more than a line extending forever into the past and future.

---

 6. For all you math buffs out there, a point at the end of a line actually makes the line into a line segment. Just to be clear.

GOD—THE ONE WHO IS

What if eternity isn't another way of saying someone lives forever into the future? What if eternity means escaping the boundaries of time entirely? God exists outside the boundaries of time.[7] He hinted at this fact in Exodus 3.

To put this scene in context, remember that Moses was 80 years old. Eighty years—that's 40 years he spent as a prince in Egypt, and then another 40 spent as a shepherd in the desert. After those 40 long years, Moses came upon an incredible sight—a bush on fire but not burning up. God spoke out of the bush, telling Moses that he was going to be sent to Pharaoh on behalf of the Israelites, who God intended to free from slavery. Moses' reaction? "Are you kidding me?"

In response, God promised He would go with Moses. Then Moses followed up with a pretty logical question:

> **"If I go to the Israelites and say to them: The God of your fathers has sent me to you, and they ask me, 'What is His name?' what should I tell them?" (Exodus 3:13).**

I have looked at this passage before and thought Moses was asking God for a secret password. Like he was going to knock on the Israelites door and they would say, "If you know God's secret name, then you can be our leader."

But that's not what Moses wanted to know. He asked God the fundamental question that plagues us if we've ever been through a period of pain, doubt, and difficulty. Moses wanted to know, "Who are You really?"[8]

It's a valid question. After all, Moses had been in the desert for 40 years with no communication from this so-called God. And he wasn't the only one waiting for God. Though God had promised the Israelites a land of their own and deliverance, they had been in back-breaking slavery to the Egyptians for 400 years. Doesn't it make sense that they would look up to the heavens with outstretched hands and say, "Are You there? Do You care? You say You are and that You do, but where are You?"

I've asked those questions before. You probably have too. They are some of the fundamental questions we ask when experiencing pain: Who are You really, God? Do You care? Are You emotionally invested in what's happening here, or do You simply rule from heaven without concern for the earth? God answered Moses. He answers us. He answered with the revelation of who He is and will always be in Exodus 3:14:

> **"I AM WHO I AM. This is what you are to say to the Israelites: I AM has sent me to you."**

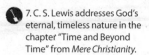 7. C. S. Lewis addresses God's eternal, timeless nature in the chapter "Time and Beyond Time" from *Mere Christianity*.

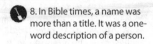 8. In Bible times, a name was more than a title. It was a one-word description of a person.

"I AM" isn't exactly a normal name, like if God had said His name was "Frank" or "Henry." In fact, what's really strange is that God's name, the summation of His character, isn't a name at all. It is, in fact, a form of the verb "to be." A more accurate translation might be, "I am the One who always is" or "I am the Is-ing One." Talk about confusing.[9]

By calling Himself "I AM," God tells us that He always is. With Him, there's no past, present, or future. He always is. He exists outside the confines of time. Because we live on the line, we can only see what is behind us, not what is far in front of us. The rules that keep us bound to the line don't apply to God—the One who created everything, including time.

OUR PRESENT TRIALS MATTER

With this new definition of eternity in mind, it makes sense how Jesus can be the Lamb slain before the foundation of the world (Revelation 13:8), or how God can treat believers like their future glorification is past tense (Romans 8:30). It's how Jesus "is the same yesterday, today, and forever" (Hebrews 13:8). And it means that when Jesus came to the earth, He temporarily bound Himself to the line of time.

God isn't just the One who was, or just the One who will be, but the One who is. To Him, everything is always right now. In God's eyes, the future is now. The past is now. Everything is now. He is the Is-ing One. As David wrote in one of his psalms of praise,

> **"From eternity to eternity the Lord's faithful love is toward those who fear Him"**
> **(Psalm 103:17).**

God's name is confirmation that eternal life with Him is an offer to escape the line of time and its effects on us. But thinking about eternity does more for us than just leave us baffled and give us hope for the future, especially when you take into account the reason behind Moses' question to begin with.

Moses struggled with his situation. And he came from a struggling people who had been slaves for 400 years. If God is the One who is, then God is invested in our present, whatever the circumstances entail. He doesn't just tell us to wait for the future or dwell on memories from the past. He's the God of right now. He's with us in our bondage. He feels our back-breaking labor. He weeps with us in our situations.

And for us, in all our junk, God is the One who Is. Not the One who will be. He's with you, and with me, personally and emotionally invested in our own "right now." He's here, and He'll always be here, because He's Yahweh, the God of the Now.

----

 9. When the word "lord" is in all capital letters in the Bible ("Lord"), it's a translation of *Yahweh*, the One Who Is. When it's written "Lord," it's a translation of *Adonai*, which can also mean "master or owner."

SESSION SIX HOLY VOCABULARY

READ. THINK. DISCUSS.

What are the differences between eternity as you've always understood it and eternity as it's described here?

What situation in your life do you need God to be the God of now?

How does knowing that He is the God of the Now change your perspective?

How does living in light of eternity change your daily experience in the world?

Why might the truth of eternity be comforting to the people around you?

6.3 HELL

Christians like to scare the hell out of people. Literally.

That effort comes in many forms and fashions. Some use the Hell House method, the Christian alternative to a haunted house on that "unmentionable" holiday in October. The idea is that people walk through a series of rooms, beginning with a scene where some teenagers are drinking alcohol, smoking cigarettes, or engaging in some other kind of debauchery. In the next room they all get in a car where, you guessed it, they meet their demise. This leads you into the "hell" room, where the heat is turned way up and you hear screaming. The message is that unless you pray a prayer, you're headed down the same path to the room with the heat.

Others stir up the fear of hell from the pulpit, by proclaiming—in the style of Jonathan Edwards' famous sermon "Sinners in the Hands of an Angry God"—that we're all dangling by a line as thin as a spider web over the abyss of eternal punishment.[10] The typical conclusion to such a sermon is that we should accept Jesus as our ticket out of the flames and pray God doesn't let go of the line.

Before we simply dismiss these tactics as "fire and brimstone" preaching, we've got to face the fact that Jesus, too, talked about hell. So did Paul. So did John in the Book of Revelation. While many theologians dismiss the idea of a literal hell, the Bible clearly presents it as a real realm with real suffering for a really long time.

SO BAD BECAUSE GOD IS SO GOOD

One of the main objections people have to hell is a question of justice. How could a so-called "loving" God justifiably punish people for all eternity (a very long time) for things done in one lifetime (a relatively short time)? To do so would be unjust, if not downright mean. One way to skirt this issue is to replace belief in a literal, eternal hell with something called *annihilationism*, the idea that at some point everyone not in heaven will simply cease to exist. No eternal life for them, but no eternal death either.

This view is fairly popular, and honestly, I can't say I'm exactly comfortable with eternal punishment either. Who really is? But just because I'm not comfortable with it doesn't mean it's not a reality. What helps me accept the reality of the extreme severity of hell isn't the meanness of God—it's His goodness.

A little story here to illustrate.

I was sort of a punk kid sometimes. I never did anything too extreme, but I certainly did some things I'm not proud of. When I was in the fifth grade, I was playing a pick-up

---

 10. Preached in 1741, this sermon is credited with sparking the Great Awakening in New England.

football game in a field. We had the "don't rush the passer" rule, so instead of actually chasing after the quarterback, all the defensive person could do was try and block the pass. It never worked, so most people would just drop back and wait. You know, play it cool.

But once when I was the quarterback, this kid who everybody thought was incredibly annoying happened to be defending me. Instead of playing it cool, he started jumping up and down and shouting at the top of his lungs. So instead of throwing the pass down the field, I threw it as hard as I could right at his face. It hit him hard, and he went down even harder. Everybody laughed because they agreed he was annoying.

Now imagine, though, if it wasn't the annoying kid defending against me as the quarterback. Imagine instead it was a 5-year-old girl eating an ice cream cone. What if I did the very same thing and with all my might smacked her in the face with a football? Even a group of fifth grade boys would have thought I was a jerk.

Isn't it interesting that the "badness" of the act changes with the "goodness" of the one the act is committed against? Same act, but different person. This is why I believe in a literal hell. Hell is so bad not only because of the bad things we do, but because we do them to a God who is so good:

> "For the LORD is good, and His love is eternal; His faithfulness endures through all generations" (Psalm 100:5).

THE SEVERITY OF OUR SINS

God isn't a 5-year-old girl. He's God. He's the Creator and Perfect Sustainer of the Universe. God isn't defined by good; good is defined by God. That's how holy and righteous He is. When we wrong Him, it's a big deal. So big because He is so good. If God were just a vindictive deity, someone waiting to zap us from heaven, then maybe sin would be a little bit justifiable. After all, that god is a jerk. Who cares if we wrong it? But that's not our God.

Perhaps the root of our inability to accept the reality of hell is because we fail to grasp the utter and complete purity and goodness of God. If we truly caught a glimpse of who He is, I believe we would cease to question the morality of sending people to hell.

Something else would happen, too. We would begin to see the true nature of sin. We would start to see rebellion against this God, who is the very definition of good, as something a little more serious than an occasional mistake or error in judgment. We would begin to understand just how greatly we've wronged God and how grievous the just punishment is for such actions.

 Visit *outofur.com* for videos on the subject of hell from some of today's leading theologians, including N. T. Wright, Erwin McManus, Tim Keller, John Piper, and others.

In short, not only would we accept the appropriate badness of hell, but we would also be convinced that we should go there. But go where, exactly?

WHERE GOD IS NOT

Most of our ideas about where hell is and what it's like don't come from the Bible. They come from authors like Dante Alighieri and John Milton, and books like *The Divine Comedy* and *Paradise Lost*. The images from those books have done far more to influence our ideas than the Bible.[11]

Jesus talked about a realm in which there is "weeping and gnashing of teeth" and "outer darkness." He also said that hell is where "their worm does not die, and the fire is not quenched."[12] The most descriptive place in Scripture where we find Jesus talking about hell is in the story of the rich man and Lazarus in Luke 16. The rich man was cast into a place where he was conscious of his surroundings and even aware of what was happening in heaven:

> **"One day the poor man died and was carried away by the angels to Abraham's side. The rich man also died and was buried. And being in torment in Hades, he looked up and saw Abraham a long way off, with Lazarus at his side" (Luke 16:22-23).**

Is hell below our feet? Is it in another dimension? We don't know, and frankly, it's not that important. The location of hell isn't its defining characteristic. Its primary characteristic is the absence of God.

Hell is so terrible not because there is fire or brimstone or endless torture. Hell is the place where God is not. All the common graces of the Lord are removed. There is no hope, no joy, no pleasure, for God is the source of these things. We have no idea what such a world would be like, because even in the worst places on earth God is still present. Rain still falls. Seasons still change. Plants grow and a host of other things happen that reveal the presence of God.

Hell has none of that. Hell is hell because God is not there. This again points us back to His absolute and complete goodness. He's the God who wrapped Himself in flesh and walked, talked, and died among us. For us. He's good. And because He's so good, hell is so, so real.

11. In 1826, nearly five centuries after Dante wrote *The Divine Comedy*, English poet William Blake illustrated the work.

12. See Matthew 8:12; 13:36-43; 22:13; 24:51; 25:30; and Mark 9:44-48.

READ. THINK. DISCUSS.

Why do you think it's important to believe in a literal hell?

What does believing in a place like hell do to the way we live day by day?

What should believing in hell motivate you to do and focus on in life?

Where does the topic of hell belong in the scope of Christian teaching?

6.4 HEAVEN

What is the Christian's ultimate destination? Most of us would readily throw our hands in the air to answer this one: "Heaven, of course!" That's where we're going. That's our trajectory. This train is, after all, bound for glory, this train . . .

But let's not be too quick to answer that question. Or at least let's not answer it without thinking about it. Yes, heaven is where we're headed. That's where Jesus is now, and thank God, He's preparing a place for us there, too:

> **"In My Father's house are many dwelling places; if not, I would have told you. I am going away to prepare a place for you. If I go away and prepare a place for you, I will come back and receive you to Myself, so that where I am you may be also" (John 14:2-3).**

Once we became Christians, heaven took the place of this world as our true home. We live the rest of our lives on earth as strangers and aliens (1 Peter 2:11).

Heaven is where death is swallowed up into life. Where justice is fully served. Where God's reign is perfectly realized without exception. In heaven, there's no more need for Kleenex.® Or chemotherapy. Or funeral processions. Or good-bye's. It's where the streets are paved with gold and the eternal worship of a multitude of Christ-followers rings for all eternity.[13]

Sounds pretty good. But are all those attributes, good as they are, really what make heaven *heaven*? The answer, maybe surprisingly, is no. Or at least, not exactly.

WHERE GOD IS FULLY KNOWN

In the same way as hell is hell because it's the realm where God is not, heaven is heaven because it's the realm where God is most fully realized. Paul pointed to this reality in 1 Corinthians 13:12:

> **"For now we see indistinctly, as in a mirror, but then face to face. Now I know in part, but then I will know fully, as I am fully known."**

Amazing. How fully known are we from God's perspective? He knows the number of hairs on our heads. He knows our deepest thoughts and motivations. He knows us, in fact, better than we know ourselves. He knows our past, present, and future. God knows us completely. Fully. Without exception.

That's how well we will know God in heaven. No matter how hard we seek after the Lord here on earth, we will always see a refracted image of Him. The image will always be in

13. The apostle John gives us a glimpse into heaven in the Book of Revelation.

some way distorted by our humanity and the imperfections of our world. But in heaven? No distortions. Perfect and complete intimacy with God Almighty.

And that's why heaven is heaven. Not because of golden streets or dried up tears. Or because of reunions with relatives or eternal worship services. Heaven is heaven because heaven is where we will really experience the fullness of joy that comes from knowing God. Jesus, too, pointed to this reality in John 17:3 when He described, in succinct form, what eternal life really is:

> "This is eternal life: that they may know You, the only true God, and the One You have sent—Jesus Christ."

That wonderful, unfiltered, perfect knowledge and intimacy of God is the essence of heaven. Our destination as Christians isn't so much to a place; it's to God Himself. In heaven, we will join in the eternal worship of God. Right now, worship is really an act of faith. Our worship is an expression of belief in the unseen and a celebration of all that we know God to be. We know Him to be those things by faith. However in heaven, worship will take on an entirely new dimension.

I'll admit it—for a long time my biggest concern about heaven was boredom. If heaven is an unending worship service, then I've worried that I'd get a little tired of singing "Shout to the Lord." But the difference between now and then is that someday, my faith won't be needed any more. As Paul said in 1 Corinthians 13:8:

> "Love never ends. But as for prophecies, they will come to an end; as for languages, they will cease; as for knowledge, it will come to an end. For we know in part, and we prophesy in part. But when the perfect comes, the partial will come to an end."

Someday, we won't have need for those other elements; all that will remain is love.[14] God's unending, matchless, extravagant love for us, and out of that, our love for Him and each other. That's what worship will be like in heaven.

BLESSED ASSURANCE

Furthermore, God is very concerned that we don't have any question about whether or not we're going to heaven. He wants us to have confidence in our destination, rather than doubt as to whether or not we're going to spend eternity with Him. That's different than the way I grew up.

I've sat through many a church service that ended like this: "I want everyone to bow their heads and close their eyes. And I want to ask you a question: If you were to die tonight, do

---

 Listen to "Waiting for My Child to Come Home" by Mavis Staples and Patty Griffin from the *Holy Vocabulary* playlist.

 14. *"Now these three remain: faith, hope, and love. But the greatest of these is love" (1 Corinthians 13:13).*

you know for sure you would go to heaven?" As a kid, I struggled with a couple of things about this gospel presentation. First of all, I never understood why everyone seemed to die at night. What if I died in the daytime? Do I still ask myself the same question?

Second—and more importantly—I struggled to maintain the assurance the preacher promised me as I lived my life week to week. But that all changed when I learned that my salvation wasn't dependent on me—not on my ability to be good enough or my ability to articulate the right kind of prayer. My salvation, and therefore my future in heaven, is completely dependent on God:

> "I am sure of this, that He who started a good work in you will carry it on to completion until the day of Christ Jesus" (Philippians 1:6).

The responsibility for carrying the good work of salvation to its completion doesn't rest on my shoulders; it rests on God's. And He's strong enough to handle it. Everything changes when we begin to truly trust in Christ for our salvation rather than trusting in ourselves. We are enabled to live with freedom and confidence, instead of fear and insecurity. In fact, Jesus means for us to start living for heaven right now.

DWELL ON HEAVEN'S REALITIES

If, indeed, our destination is into the presence of God (for He is the reason heaven is heaven), then the journey there begins in this life. It begins with practicing His presence in the here and now, seeking hard after the knowledge of Him, and becoming more intimate with Him each passing moment of each passing day.

Part of that process is turning our mind's attention and our heart's affection upon the realities of heaven. Paul especially was concerned that we think about heavenly things. He wrote in Colossians 3:1-3:

> "So if you have been raised with the Messiah, seek what is above, where the Messiah is, seated at the right hand of God. Set your minds on what is above, not on what is on the earth. For you have died, and your life is hidden with the Messiah in God."

I guess you could argue that thinking about the reality of heaven keeps us from focusing on the reality of life. In a way, you could say that thinking on heaven is a way to medicate ourselves from our pain on this earth. But I don't think so. I don't think God would prescribe medication like that. Here are a few reasons I see profit in spending regular time dwelling on heaven's realities.

1. To keep us from loving our stuff. Hearses don't pull UHaul® trailers, and funeral suits don't have pockets. Heaven is better anyway, so do I really need a new shirt? Or a Vespa®?

2. To provide hope. God knows we need it. That's what Paul illustrated in Romans 8. He held up his sufferings, which were many, and said that the glory that awaits us makes these afflictions pale in comparison.

3. To motivate us to action. Heaven is a place where the rule of God is recognized fully and completely. We are supposed to pray, and act, in such a way as to bring God's will about on earth as it is in heaven. If we spend time thinking about how things will be, then we can be moved to change the way things are.

4. To remind us just who we're surrounded by. C. S. Lewis reminded us in *The Weight of Glory,* "You have never talked to a mere mortal. . . . But it is immortals whom we joke with, work with, marry, snub, and exploit."[15] Dwelling on heaven makes us realize the importance of the people around us. They are immortal, and they should be treated with respect and dignity.

Let's dwell in faith on what waits for us. Little by little, we'll see ourselves transformed into the kind of people who put away the things of the earth because of our overwhelming confidence in the greatness of God—that He is better than all else.

READ. THINK. DISCUSS.

What are some other reasons it would profit you to regularly think on the realities of heaven?

Why do you think Jesus described eternal life as knowing God?

How important should heaven be to the daily life of the Christ-follower?

What do you think a person is like who regularly dwells on the reality of heaven?

15. C. S. Lewis, *The Weight of Glory* (San Francisco: Harper Collins, 2001), 46.

6.5 GLORIFICATION

It's hard not to have a Hallmark® picture of heaven in my mind. A place where people lazily drift from cloud to cloud, everyone wears diapers like tiny cherubs, and everything's in hazy slow motion. I also imagine a lot of fog, for some reason, and a dream-like feel. Everything is ethereal; nothing is concrete.

If heaven is the dwelling place of the Creator of everything, though, wouldn't it make sense for heaven to be more real, not less real, than the temporary world we live in now? This world is our only frame of reference for reality, so it's next to impossible to imagine a place more real than this, where rocks are harder, colors are more vivid, and water is more fluid. But that's what I'm banking on heaven being like.[16]

The apostle John includes a detail in his Gospel that leads us to believe this might be the case. The disciples cowered in the upper room after witnessing the crucifixion of Jesus. Not only were they grieving their friend's death, but they also felt like the past three years of their lives were a waste. Everything their Rabbi promised about being the Messiah who would lead them and rule with peace now seemed impossible. And all the dreams they shared with Him were buried underneath the two-ton rock that sealed up His body. No doubt those were dark, fearful days. Until . . .

> "In the evening of that first day of the week, the disciples were gathered together with the doors locked because of their fear of the Jews. Then Jesus came, stood among them, and said to them, 'Peace to you!'" (John 20:19).

Jesus came and stood among them, but how did He get past the locked door? A locked door is no problem for the Son of God, but I'm particularly interested in the "how" in this case. Perhaps Jesus, in His post-resurrection state, was like Hallmark heaven. Transparent, floating around, not really a solid figure anymore. That would enable Him to pass through the locked door effortlessly, like a ghost.

But what if the opposite is true? Maybe Jesus became the very definition of reality in His post-resurrection state. He was more solid, more real, than any other human being. And so He passed through the door not because He was hazy, but because it was. It was transparent. It was cloudy and without definition. It was the lesser reality. If that is true, then Jesus' glorified state was more real than earth, and Scripture tells us we can expect the same change.

FOLLOWING JESUS' LEAD

The third stage of God's work of salvation in our lives is known as glorification. When we become Christians we are *justified*—our sinful nature is replaced by Jesus' righteousness.

----

 16. That's what C. S. Lewis thought, too, and espoused in the great little book *The Great Divorce*.

 Listen to "I'll Fly Away" by Alison Krauss & Gillian Welch from the *Holy Vocabulary* playlist.

Then, through the ongoing work of the Holy Spirit in our lives, we become *sanctified*, or more Christ-like. Our sanctification continues until the point of glorification. *Glorification* is the final work of God in our lives, and it has two parts. First, is the perfection of our souls when we die and enter into God's presence:

> **"The Spirit Himself testifies together with our spirit that we are God's children, and if children, also heirs—heirs of God and co-heirs with Christ—seeing that we suffer with Him so that we may also be glorified with Him" (Romans 8:16-17).**

The second part of our glorification will take place when Jesus returns and we receive our resurrected, perfected bodies like He did after His resurrection:

> **"For if the dead are not raised, Christ has not been raised. And if Christ has not been raised, your faith is worthless; you are still in your sins" (1 Corinthians 15:16-17).**[17]

A few verses later, Paul refers to Jesus as "the firstfruits of those who have fallen asleep" (1 Corinthians 15:20). The firstfruits are the beginning; the best of a crop. But they are also symbolic of the nature of what the entire crop is going to yield. Jesus' resurrection is an example of His being the firstfruit—He's the first among us to be glorified, but we will follow His example.

NO SUCH THING AS PERFECT . . . YET

In 2 Corinthians 5 Paul discussed the conflict between our current physical state and the perfected one to come:

> **"For we know that if our earthly house, a tent, is destroyed, we have a building from God, a house not made with hands, eternal in the heavens. And, in fact, we groan in this one, longing to put on our house from heaven, since, when we are clothed, we will not be found naked. Indeed, we who are in this tent groan, burdened as we are, because we do not want to be unclothed but clothed, so that mortality may be swallowed up by life" (2 Corinthians 5:1-4).**

That's great language. Right now we languish in tents, but true homes await us. Our bodies are like canvas portables, flapping in the breeze of disease and decay. But even our daily physical decay is a reminder that something better is just around the corner. With Christ as our forerunner, we are waiting for the time when we will enter into eternal life, rather than death. Our bodies literally groan in anticipation of perfection.

Whether we like to admit it or not, we live in a constant state of decay. Our bodies aren't getting better; they're getting worse. We've been dying since the first time we cried in our moms' arms. But the great truth of the gospel is that death is really the doorway into true

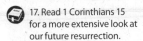

17. Read 1 Corinthians 15 for a more extensive look at our future resurrection.

life. It's as if right now we're in a stage production with elaborately designed sets depicting the mountains, rivers, and trees. Death is the doorway that we use to exit stage right, and when we do, we find ourselves outside in the real nature. No imitations. No pale reflections. Only the greatest embodiment of reality.

HOPE IN WHAT'S TO COME

But glorification isn't just about our bodies; it's about our spirits as well. For the Christ-follower, every day is a struggle. We battle the sin, sadness, and circumstantial pain in our own lives. But in our glorified state, there will be no more fighting through struggles. Sin will be a distant memory, because in that state, we will fully realize the new people God has made us in Christ. In glorification, we won't have any competing desires to our want of Jesus. We'll find in Him an inexhaustible well of pleasure and goodness.

In the meantime, though, the Christian life is a study in contradictions.[18] We are children of God, and co-heirs of the kingdom with Christ, yet we have allergies. And diseases. And car wrecks. And depression. Paul gets at this contradiction in Romans 8:

> "Who can separate us from the love of Christ? Can affliction or anguish or persecution or famine or nakedness or danger of sword? As it is written: Because of You we are being put to death all day long; we are counted as sheep to be slaughtered. No, in all these things we are more than victorious through Him who loved us" (Romans 8:35-37).

See the contradiction? We are inseparably loved by God in Christ. We are super-conquerors.[19] Still, we face death and destruction from all sides all day long. In fact, the world might look at Christians and say, "You can't be loved by God. Look at your lives! Look at how you suffer!"

The reality is that we are not the sum of our circumstances. We are more. And though we don't look like glorified children of God now, someday we will. One day Jesus will return, but He won't come back in an unassuming manner. There won't be any nondescript mangers and anonymous towns. He'll split the sky and reveal Himself as the King of the universe.

On that day, when the entire universe sees Jesus as He truly is, our real identity will also be revealed. Finally, our outer selves will match our inner reality. Our bodies, minds, and spirits will be made perfect and complete.

---

 18. As we mentioned in "5.2 Kingdom" (page 106), we're the people of the already but not yet.

 19. The phrase "more than conquerors" was made up by Paul. This is the only place it appears in Scripture.

READ. THINK. DISCUSS.

How do you see the decay of death in your own body?

Where do you see the spark of your identity as God's child in your body?

How does considering your future glorification change your attitude about the present?

Have you ever considered that heaven will be more real than earth? How does that change your daily approach to your circumstances?

SCRIPTURE

the beginning was the word, and the
with god and the word was god. He wa
the beginning. Through Him all things
; without him nothing was made that
made In him was life, and that li
ight of men the light shines in the

GOD'S WORD FOR US IN SCRIPTURE

Every club has a rule book, some kind of guide that establishes a code of conduct all members of said club are expected to abide by. Take the Boy Scouts for example. Boy Scouts are expected to have the *Boy Scout Handbook* memorized. It helps one learn how to survive on wilderness adventures, but it also details how Boy Scouts should present themselves to the world. As a Boy Scout, you are the face of the organization and portray its values to the world. Naturally, the Boy Scouts of America want all their members on the same page. Thus, the *Boy Scout Handbook*.

Is that all the Bible is? The Christian's version of the *Boy Scout Handbook*?

As people of faith, we treat this book with great reverence. We consider it the Word of God, the authoritative definition of truth, and the record of God's revelation of Himself to the world. Yes, it sets the standard for how we are to live our lives, but it also provides us with the basis for what we know about God and ourselves. Everything we believe is rooted in the words of Scripture.

But how can we be so confident in this book? What does it mean that Scripture is "God-breathed" and holds authority in our lives? What place does Jesus have in the Bible story? How does the inspiration of the Holy Spirit work? And what separates this book from all the other works of literature produced over the course of history?

These are important questions to answer, not only because they bolster our faith as Christians, but also because they help us know exactly what we're believing when we trust the Bible. If we fail to answer those questions, we aren't really thinking about the fundamental beliefs we have about the universe. Instead, we're simply imitating what others have taught us without thinking through the implications.

Fortunately, the Bible is up to the challenge of being picked apart. It has much to say about itself. It confirms our beliefs in its authority and strengthens our resolve about its source. Through reading, memorizing, and processing what the Bible says and the implications of its content, we come to understand that this isn't just another book on our shelves.

The Bible is much, much more.

7.1 GOD-BREATHED

God is not aloof. Sometimes we think He is, especially when things in our lives seem to be spiraling out of control. We look up at the sky and shake our fist toward heaven crying, "Where are You? Why don't You do something?"

Far from being distant, though, the Bible offers continual evidence of God's desire for intimacy and community. Before God, in His divine creativity, thought up the concept of time, iguanas, or the spinal column, He existed in perfect community with Himself in the confines of the Trinity.[1] Then the intimacy between the Father, Son, and Spirit overflowed into His creation.

God didn't plop Adam and Eve into the garden and tell them He'd be back to check on them in a couple of years. Instead, He walked and talked with them in the cool of the day. After He delivered His people from Egyptian bondage, He specifically instructed them to build an elaborate but portable tent so He could dwell in the midst of His people. And if we fast forward to the very end of time, when heaven comes down to meet earth, the resounding cry echoes this desire:

> **"Look! God's dwelling is with men, and He will live with them. They will be His people, and God Himself will be with them and be their God" (Revelation 21:3).**

At its core, Christianity is an experience of God's revelation of Himself, driven by His desire to be known intimately by His people. He already knows us inside and out since He knitted us together in our mothers' wombs (Psalm 139:13). For us to know Him, however, requires revelation. Through nature, we can glean certain things about God we know to be true, but that's a limited degree of knowledge about Him. And that's not sufficient for His children. He wants to be known fully and completely, for He knows that knowing Him is the pathway for humanity to experience the greatest amount of joy imaginable. Out of His love for us, God has revealed Himself to us. God has given us the greatest gift in the universe in His divine revelation.

SPIRIT-LED OR OUT OF CONTROL?

There, right in the middle of God's desire to be known, we find the Bible. The Bible is the record of God's self-revelation. As such, it is no mere book. Scripture (which literally means "writings") is inspired. Or to take a phrase from Paul, it is "God-breathed."[2] Jesus certainly regarded it as such. In the great story of His temptation in the wilderness, when Satan tempted Him with power and self-reliance, Jesus responded by quoting Scripture:

> **"Man must not live on bread alone but on every word that comes from the mouth of God" (Matthew 4:4).**

---

 1. Read John 17 for a closer look at the intimate bond between the Trinity.

 2. "God-breathed" is the translation of *theopneustos* in 2 Timothy 3:16 (NIV). Another translation is "inspired by God."

Along with Jesus and Paul, Peter was also convinced of the divine source of Scripture. He wrote,

> **"You should know this: no prophecy of Scripture comes from one's own interpretation, because no prophecy ever came by the will of man; instead, moved by the Holy Spirit, men spoke from God" (2 Peter 1:20-21).**

In the same way God breathed life into Adam, He breathed Himself into the biblical authors and their words. But how does that work? Was David just sitting there one day, minding his own business, when he fell into a trance, only to wake up hours later and find the 23rd Psalm written on paper in front of him?

Some say that's precisely what happened. The authors of Scripture literally lost control of themselves and just started writing. But I'm not sure Scripture itself confirms that take on divine inspiration.

For example, consider the first few verses of the Book of Acts:

> **"I wrote the first narrative, Theophilus, about all that Jesus began to do and teach until the day He was taken up, after He had given orders through the Holy Spirit to the apostles whom He had chosen" (Acts 1:1-2).**

That's how Dr. Luke began his record of the acts of the early church. In his opening thoughts, we see a few things that help us know how the "God-breathed" component of scriptural authorship worked. Luke had a specific intent. He wanted to document a logical recording of factual events. And he was sending his work to someone special, maybe a high-ranking official in the government.[3] We also know that the Book of Acts is the sequel to the story he began in the Gospel of Luke.

In fact, if we flip back to part one of Luke's story, we find similar language:

> **"Many have undertaken to compile a narrative about the events that have been fulfilled among us, just as the original eyewitnesses and servants of the word handed them down to us. It also seemed good to me, since I have carefully investigated everything from the very first, to write to you in orderly sequence, most honorable Theophilus, so that you may know the certainty of the things about which you have been instructed" (Luke 1:1-4).**

Specific person. Specific purpose. Specific point in history. Luke didn't lose control; he wrote with a clear head. In our understanding of Scripture, we must understand that every sentence in the Bible was written within a specific context to a specific group of people.

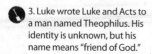

3. Luke wrote Luke and Acts to a man named Theophilus. His identity is unknown, but his name means "friend of God."

But that doesn't diminish the work of God in it. It simply means that the Holy Spirit chose to work through the events of the times and the personalities of the writers to pen the revelation of God found in the Bible.

PERSPECTIVE MATTERS

Let's consider the four Gospels as another example of God's inspiration of Scripture. Ever wonder why there are four Gospels and not just one? Or why some record events that others leave out? Why some are ordered chronologically and others ordered thematically? Why the Christmas story is a big deal in some but not in others?

We might be tempted to look at these questions and others and doubt the inspiration of Scripture, for surely the Holy Spirit would inspire all four writers to write exactly the same thing. But that notion fails to account for God's desire to be glorified in diversity. The various personalities of the Gospel writers is one example of how He has chosen to display that diversity in Scripture.

If you read Luke, you're going to get a very logical retelling of the events of Jesus' life. And though you can't pigeon-hole people in regards to Scripture, I guess you could say this Gospel might appeal to the accountant—one who is meticulous, ordered, and careful. What about an artist, someone with a completely different personality type? The artist may not resonate as much with Luke. John, on the other hand, is full of flowery language and vivid pictures—a creative type can really sink his or her teeth into that. It's less like a newspaper article and more like an abstract painting.

Each Gospel tells the same story as viewed from four different perspectives, which means we get a more complete picture of what's going on.

Imagine there was a car crash in the middle of an intersection. Four people were standing on opposite corners and all witnessed the accident. The officer on the scene would want to interview all four of them because their individual vantage points would give the best, most accurate, and most detailed picture possible. Such is the case with the Word of God.

We don't find 66 books in the Bible telling separate stories, but one complete record of the revelation of God, told through a variety of different viewpoints. That variety helps to enhance the ultimate aim of Scripture—to know God.

That's right—the ultimate aim of the Bible is to help us know God. It's not to help us live a good life. We do the God-breathed words of the Bible a disservice when we approach them primarily as a tool rather than the story of God. Yes there are principles in Scripture that teach us how to walk rightly, but all its principles are meant to be seen in light of the

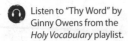 Listen to "Thy Word" by Ginny Owens from the *Holy Vocabulary* playlist.

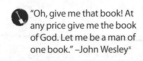 "Oh, give me that book! At any price give me the book of God. Let me be a man of one book." –John Wesley[x]

overarching purpose of the Bible. Namely, that we might be intimately acquainted with the One who so passionately wants to be intimately acquainted with us.

READ. THINK. DISCUSS.

In your own words, what does it mean that the Bible is God-breathed? How does this shape the way you approach Scripture?

What are three words you would use to describe your general attitude about the Bible?

Why do you think it's difficult to regularly read the Bible?

How important is Scripture memory to you? Why?

Do you see the Bible as a tool or as a revelation? What's the difference?

7.2 AUTHORITY

You could say that our culture has an authority problem. Fifty years ago, respect for authority was the rule rather than the exception. If you don't believe me, try having a lengthy conversation with a grandparent on any given topic and a healthy respect for authority will become evident. Job titles like president, senator, general, or reverend used to be enough to demand people be treated with authority. The reasoning was simple: Somebody thought enough of those people to put them in positions of authority so they could be respected and trusted.

Respect for authority has eroded in the span of a few decades because of a lack of trust. People used to trust their authorities, then their authorities betrayed them (at least in popular opinion). People looked at Watergate, the Vietnam War, and scandals in the personal lives of government officials as evidence of the abuse of authority and the betrayal of public trust.

In our own day, Enron and the Wall Street collapse haven't done much to remedy that distrust. Combine that with the litany of stories from the evangelical world of leaders' extramarital affairs and financial embezzlement and you get a culture burnt out on authority.

In addition to the trust issue, we tend to see authority as an encroachment on our freedom to do what we want, when we want. We are the captains of our own ships; the masters of our own destinies. If someone has authority, it means he or she is in a position to wield power and command over things, but we don't like anyone—or anything, for that matter—to have power over us. In no way are we going to let someone tell us how to live.

Authority is a word that comes up frequently when people talk about Scripture. When we say the Bible has authority in our lives, we mean what's written in it establishes truth and determines how we are to live as Christians. But how can the Bible do that? And how do we not allow our personal authority issues to conflict with the role God's Word is supposed to play in our lives?

GOD'S AUTHORITY IN BOOK FORM

At the root of our objections to authority is our sense of entitlement. We believe we have the right to do anything we want to do, and we're ready to cry "foul" the moment someone or something infringes on those rights. We're kidding ourselves if we think that's true. We were purposefully imagined and crafted into being by the God of the universe. He's the One who made us, so His is the ultimate authority in our lives.

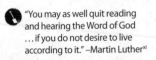

"You may as well quit reading and hearing the Word of God … if you do not desire to live according to it." –Martin Luther[xi]

SESSION SEVEN HOLY VOCABULARY

When being sentenced to death, Jesus reminded Pilate of God's authority over everything, even Pilate's governance:

> "Pilate said to Him, 'You're not talking to me? Don't You know that I have the authority to release You and the authority to crucify You?' 'You would have no authority over Me at all,' Jesus answered him, 'if it hadn't been given you from above. This is why the one who handed Me over to you has the greater sin'" (John 19:10-11).

As the One who made everything, God is really the only being in all the universe who can rightly claim "rights." He's the One with all the authority, and the Bible, as God's Word, carries that authority in its pages.[4]

That means that the Bible isn't just a book. It's not like *Poor Richard's Almanac* or another book of wise sayings. It doesn't contain merely suggestions or advice. To say the Bible has authority is to recognize its great differences from other books. Hebrews 4:12-13 points this fact out:

> "For the word of God is living and effective and sharper than any two-edged sword, penetrating as far as to divide soul, spirit, joints, and marrow; it is a judge of the ideas and thoughts of the heart. No creature is hidden from Him, but all things are naked and exposed to the eyes of Him to whom we must give an account."

Paul also applied the sword imagery to God's Word when he described the metaphorical armor Christians should be clothed in to fight off the false authorities—the devil and "the spiritual forces of evil"—at work in the world:

> "Take up the full armor of God, so that you may be able to resist in the evil day, and having prepared everything, to take your stand. Stand, therefore, with truth like a belt around your waist, righteousness like armor on your chest, and your feet sandaled with readiness for the gospel of peace. In every situation take the shield of faith, and with it you will be able to extinguish the flaming arrows of the evil one. Take the helmet of salvation, *and the sword of the Spirit, which is God's word*" (Ephesians 6:13-17, emphasis added).

That's pretty vivid imagery, but anyone who has spent time digging into Scripture knows it's true. Through the power of the Holy Spirit, we find that when we go to the Bible to read it, it actually reads us. We see ourselves measured against its commands. Our true motivations are revealed in its characters. And the goodness and grace of the gospel drips off its pages.

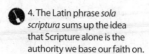
4. The Latin phrase *sola scriptura* sums up the idea that Scripture alone is the authority we base our faith on.

THE MEASURING STICK FOR TRUTH

We live in a culture that thinks truth is relative and subjective; not only is there no such thing as absolute truth, but those who attest to it are arrogant to think so. Yet in Christianity, we not only believe that there is absolute truth, but that the Bible is its measuring stick.

There are a lot of different apologetic and philosophical arguments one might make for such bold assertions, but just consider this one: If you found a copy of a Shakespearean play lying around, you might pick it up and read it. You might enjoy it and find the language beautiful. But you're probably not going to stop reading it, get a girlfriend, and arrange an elaborate hoax of your deaths in order to be together. You might appreciate *Romeo and Juliet*, but you're not going to order your life around it.

Yet that's precisely what has happened with the Bible for thousands of years. As it's been translated into language after language and brought to culture after culture, the reaction has been the same—people turning from entire ways of life and belief systems to embrace the ultimate truth of God in Jesus Christ.

The fact that the Bible is the measuring stick for truth has special relevance for us as Christians because of the challenge to hear the voice of God clearly in our lives. We might think God is telling us this or that, but is it really His voice we're hearing? Or are we being influenced by things that contradict His truth? Through the words of Scripture, the voice of the Lord is authenticated. I confidently believe God speaks to us, but I also believe He has spoken, and He's not going to contradict Himself.

The Bible is how we separate the voice of God from the voices around us (and in our heads for that matter). Any message we think we've received from the Lord must be able to hold up against the standard of truth in the Bible. If the two align, there's a much better chance the Lord has indeed spoken.

Embracing the authority of Scripture doesn't confine us. It doesn't encroach on our freedom. Rather, it gives us the freedom to fully follow God with our whole hearts. It lets us freely hear from Him and act with confidence in His will. And, as the apostle Paul reminded the Romans, God's Word serves as a reminder that He is who He says He is, and in Him we have hope:

> **"For whatever was written before was written for our instruction, so that through our endurance and through the encouragement of the Scriptures we may have hope"** (Romans 15:4).

If we read it, that is.

READ. THINK. DISCUSS.

Who holds authority in your life? What does it mean to submit to their authority?

What would it be like to regard the Bible as having no authority? What would Scripture become to you?

How is the Bible the measuring stick of all truth?

Do you need to change how you relate to the Bible in order to reflect its authority? Explain.

7.3 JESUS

Really? Jesus? That seems like a misplaced topic for a section on Scripture. But the truth is, we can't understand the intent and the story of the Bible without looking at Jesus' role in it. In the earlier session on Christ, we defined Jesus as the Son of God, both fully divine and fully human, whose death and resurrection on the cross satisfied God's justice on our behalf. We learn all about Jesus and His work through Scripture, but there's more to it than that.

THE MAIN CHARACTER OF SCRIPTURE

The apostle John begins His Gospel by defining Jesus' relationship to Scripture:

> **"In the beginning was the Word, and the Word was with God, and the Word was God" (John 1:1).**

A few verses later we read,

> **"The Word became flesh and took up residence among us. We observed His glory, the glory as the One and Only Son from the Father, full of grace and truth" (John 1:14).**

Simply put, Jesus is the Word of God. He is God's message of self-revelation to the world. We read the Bible to learn about God and who we are as His children, and in doing so we see Jesus. As Jesus put it:

> **"If you know Me, you will also know My Father . . ." (John 14:7).**

While Jesus was on earth, His opponents argued that He stood in opposition to the holy Scriptures and had no respect for the Jewish (Old Testament) laws. They couldn't have been further from the truth. Jesus is the perfect fulfillment of every one of God's laws and all the claims of God's prophets. When He described Himself in this way in Matthew 5:17-18, Jesus went so far as to say that nothing in Scripture was nullified by His coming. Not even "the smallest letter or one stroke of a letter" would disappear from Scripture.[5]

The high standards of God's law, described in the Pentateuch (the first five books of the Bible) are unattainable by sinful humans. But by living among us in perfect obedience to that law, Jesus freed us from it and grants us the righteousness the law required. The author of Hebrews said it best:

> **"How much more will the blood of the Messiah, who through the eternal Spirit offered Himself without blemish to God, cleanse our consciences from dead**

 5. This phrase refers to the Hebrew letter *yod*. It's roughly the same size as an apostrophe.

 "The Bible is to me the most precious thing in the world just because it tells me the story of Jesus." –George MacDonald[xii]

works to serve the living God? Therefore He is the mediator of a new covenant, so that those who are called might receive the promise of the eternal inheritance, because a death has taken place for redemption from the transgressions committed under the first covenant" (Hebrews 9:14-15).[6]

Jesus fulfills the law because He perfectly kept it; not only in action, but in motive. Not only in deed, but in heart. We don't get to be righteous people by climbing the ladder of the law; we get to be righteous people by exchanging our sin for the righteousness of Christ.[7]

Jesus' fulfillment of God's law on our behalf shows one aspect of His role in Scripture. Beyond that, as the Word of God, Jesus is the main character of Scripture. He's not just the protagonist of the Gospels, or the One who's being foreshadowed in the Old Testament law passages. Turn to any page of the Bible, and whether you read about the dietary codes of Leviticus, the praises of the Psalms, the locusts of Joel, or the crazy tattoos of Revelation, dig a little bit and you'll find Jesus. I promise, He's there.

THE ONE TRUE HERO

One interesting way we see Jesus in all of Scripture is through realizing that none of the other characters are heroes. Have you ever noticed that? Pick any biblical character who we tend to treat as a heroic figure and you will read about their failings:

DAVID: A man after God's own heart, a talented songwriter, and the greatest king Israel had. He was a faithful friend, a tremendous leader, and impressive with a slingshot. He was also a bad father, an adulterer, and a murderer.

MOSES: Scripture calls him the most humble man who ever lived (Numbers 12:3). He spoke with God face to face, and he stood up to the most powerful leader on the planet and boldly proclaimed the word of the Lord. He also killed a man and was prevented from entering the promised land due to his brashness and lack of faith.

ABRAHAM: He was the father of God's chosen people, and even when the New Testament was written, he was considered a model of faith. He didn't withhold his long-awaited son from the Lord but offered him up as a sacrifice. But he also believed in God so little that he passed off his wife as his sister for fear of being killed by the Egyptians.

The list goes on. Peter denied being Jesus' friend. Samson loved pagan women. Gideon was a coward. When reading these stories, we can't help but recognize the abject humanity of their characters. The Bible stories don't portray any characters in a purely heroic light. Why might that be?

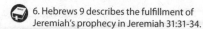 6. Hebrews 9 describes the fulfillment of Jeremiah's prophecy in Jeremiah 31:31-34.

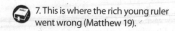 7. This is where the rich young ruler went wrong (Matthew 19).

I believe it's because we are meant to see Jesus as the center and the hero of every story, even the ones in which He seems absent. We can relate to the imperfections and mistakes the most important characters in Scripture made. They look a lot like the mistakes we make (or worse, even). But all the ways these obedient people of God failed to be perfect highlight Jesus' perfection. Their mistakes leave no doubt that Jesus alone was able to be our hero, God's perfect sacrifice on behalf of all our errs.

THE PERFECTION OF EVERY STORY

In addition to being the One true hero of the Bible, Jesus is the perfection of every story. Each story in the Bible reveals part of His character and helps paint a complete picture of who Jesus is and how He works in our lives. Pastor and author Timothy Keller gives us a list of just a few of the places in the Bible where we learn things about Jesus' character and ministry, other than what's written in the Gospels:[8]

- Jesus is the true and better Adam, who passed the test in the garden and whose obedience is imputed to us.
- Jesus is the true and better Abel, who, though innocently slain, has blood now that cries out not for our condemnation, but for our acquittal.
- Jesus is the true and better Abraham, who answered the call of God to leave all the comfortable and familiar, and go out into the void, not knowing whither he went, to create a new people of God.
- Jesus is the true and better Isaac, who was not just offered up by His Father on the mount, but was truly sacrificed for us. And when God said to Abraham, "now I know you love Me, because you did not withhold your son, your only son whom you love from Me," now we can look at God, taking His Son up the mountain and sacrificing Him, and say, "now we know that You love us, because You did not withhold Your Son, Your only Son whom You love from us."
- Jesus is the true and better Jacob, who wrestled and took the blow of justice we deserve, so we, like Jacob, only receive the wounds of grace to wake us up and discipline us.
- Jesus is the true and better Joseph, who at the right hand of the king, forgives those who betrayed and sold Him, and uses His new power to save them.
- Jesus is the true and better Moses, who stands in the gap between the people and the Lord, and who mediates a new covenant.
- Jesus is the true and better rock of Moses, who was struck with the rod of God's justice, and now gives us water in the desert.
- Jesus is the true and better Job, the truly innocent sufferer who then intercedes for and saves His stupid friends.
- Jesus is the true and better David, whose victory becomes His people's victory though they never lifted a stone to accomplish it themselves.
- Jesus is the true and better Esther, who didn't just risk losing an earthly palace, but lost the ultimate and heavenly one, who didn't just risk His life, but gave His life to save His people.

 8. Explore these individual stories on your own to see for yourself Jesus' centrality in Scripture.

- Jesus is the true and better Jonah, who was cast out into the storm so we could be brought in.
- He is the real Passover Lamb, innocent, perfect, helpless, slain so that the angel of death would pass over us.[9]

Once you start to look for Jesus in Scripture, you see Him everywhere. *Everywhere.* We are like the two men walking on the road to Emmaus who encountered Jesus but didn't recognize Him. They didn't recognize Him until He opened their eyes to see Him throughout all Scripture:

> **"Then beginning with Moses and all the Prophets, He interpreted for them the things concerning Himself in all the Scriptures" (Luke 24:27).**

Open your Bible. Jesus is there, on every page, walking beside you.

READ. THINK. DISCUSS.

Do you believe there are no heroes in the Bible? Can you think of any reasons, other than Jesus' role as hero, that might be the case?

What do you think of Jesus being the central character in Scripture? What makes accepting that truth most difficult for you?

How do the ideas in this section impact the way you should read Scripture?

Think about your own favorite story from the Bible. Can you find Jesus there? Where?

 9. This list is from Timothy Keller's sermon "Gospel-Centered Ministry." Listen to the sermon at *theresurgence.com*.

7.4 LAW

Rules, rules, rules. For a religion that's supposed to be about grace, it's hard to escape the fact that when you open the Bible, you find so many rules. Rules about worship. Rules about sacrifices. Rules about marriage. Rules about parenting. Rules about money. And those are just the common ones.

You also find rules about mildew. Rules about eating. And even rules about where to go to the bathroom when you're camping. There's no getting around it—Scripture is full of rules. Many of these rules are listed in the Old Testament, in the section of the Bible that is commonly called the Law.

Generally, when people talk about the Books of the Law, they mean the first five books of the Old Testament, or the Pentateuch. Written by Moses, the Pentateuch contains God's ordinances to the fledgling nation of Israel as they were reestablishing themselves as a nation after being freed from slavery. The Law is the record of God's specific directives about how His people were supposed to live every area of their lives.

But that's Old Testament stuff, right? Perhaps when we read the New Testament we'll get more of the whole grace thing. But when you turn the page between Malachi (the last book of the Old Testament) and Matthew (the first book of the New Testament and the beginning of Jesus' ministry), you don't see the law disappearing. If anything, you see that in the 400 years between Testaments, the centrality of the Law in Jewish life was heightened.

A COMPLEX WEB OF RULES

By the time of Jesus, the Jews had codified all the Old Testament Scriptures so that they had 613 laws.[10] But in order to make sure every situation was covered, they added hundreds of sub-rules, regulations, and traditions so that even the most minute area of life was covered by some arm of the law.

For example, take the law regarding work on the Sabbath, as stated in Exodus 31:15:

> **"For six days work may be done, but on the seventh day there must be a Sabbath of complete rest, dedicated to the LORD. Anyone who does work on the Sabbath day must be put to death."**

The law God originally gave Moses was plain and simple—absolutely no work is to be done on the Sabbath. But what does it really mean to work?

The Rabbis wanted to figure that out, so they divided "work" into 39 categories. One specific labor forbidden on the Sabbath was plowing. But a person didn't even have to use

---

 10. The *Talmud* is a sacred Jewish book that expands on the rabbinic laws and customs of the Old Testament.

SESSION SEVEN HOLY VOCABULARY

a plow to break this rule. If a person stood up from a chair and the legs made a furrow in the ground, he was guilty of plowing and therefore guilty of breaking the Sabbath.

You can imagine that after centuries of codifying the law, of regulating and breaking down its tiniest details, obeying it was virtually impossible. Unfortunately, when Jesus came on the scene, He didn't exactly simplify things.

In the Sermon on the Mount, Jesus very clearly said that He didn't come to abolish the law.[11] If anything, the Sermon on the Mount increased the ethical demands of the law. People walked to the hillside that day thinking murder was about the physical act of taking someone's life. But after a few minutes with Jesus, they heard that you can also commit murder in your heart by thinking ill of another.

STAIRWAY TO HEAVEN

The demands of the law set an impossible standard. We can't help but ask: If it's impossible for anyone to obey every letter of God's law, what is its purpose? Does the law exist just to remind us how bad we are, to make sure that we never get too big for our britches? Or perhaps it's there because God likes to watch us squirm underneath its weight, trying like ants to lift something that's too heavy for our bodies.

Before we talk about what the law is for, let's clarify what it's not for. The law is not, and never has been, the means of salvation and merit before God. As the apostle Paul wrote:

> "What then can we say that Abraham, our forefather according to the flesh, has found? If Abraham was justified by works, then he has something to brag about—but not before God. For what does the Scripture say? Abraham believed God, and it was credited to him for righteousness" (Romans 4:1-3).

To put it another way, God never intended that man use the law like a ladder, which is exactly what Christians have tried to do throughout human history.

A ladder is a useful tool to reach something high up. One rung at a time, you climb a ladder until you finally reach a new plane where you can at last reach what you're grasping for. In this approach to the law, God's rules form a ladder to salvation. As we keep each rule, we move one rung closer to a relationship with God.

One of the implications of that line of thinking would be that the death of Jesus was God's backup plan. If that was true, His initial plan would have been for people to keep all the regulations set before them, and therefore save themselves. But when God saw that wasn't going to happen, there was a heavenly scramble and He came up with the idea of the cross.

 11. Quite the opposite, in fact. In Matthew 5:17, Jesus said He came to fulfill the Law and the Prophets.

But God never needed a backup plan. Jesus' work on the cross was the plan from the beginning, and the law was always a part of that plan. The question, then, is how the law works together with Jesus in God's singular plan of salvation.

THE GRACE OF GOD

If the law is a ladder, then we could save ourselves by our own effort. We could achieve greatness, and at the top of the ladder we would have ourselves to pat on the back for our effort. But in climbing that ladder, it's inevitable that we would get really, really tired. Eventually we wouldn't be able to put one more hand or foot up to the next rung, and we'd end up just letting go. Unfortunately, most Christians go through an endless cycle of climbing until they're exhausted, falling off, then getting right back on again.

God never intended for us to use the law in this way, as the means of elevating ourselves to His standard. If anything, the opposite is true. The law's purpose isn't to lift us up; it's to force us down. Instead of thinking of the law as a ladder, we should think of it as a pane of glass. Glass can be clear and used as a window, or it can be polished and used as a mirror. Likewise, the law serves as both a window and a mirror in our relationship with God.

The law is a window through which we view the character of God. By looking at the law, we see the absolute moral perfection of our Creator. We observe His spotlessness and purity by looking at the standard He gave in the law. But as we do so, the other purpose of the law comes into focus. For when confronted with the law, we are forced to admit our absolute sinfulness and moral bankruptcy. In this way, the law serves as a mirror to show us how dramatically short of God's standard we fall.[12]

The law was never meant to be the means by which we are saved. Rather, the law brings us to the absolute end of ourselves, revealing how desperate we are for a Savior. In light of the law, we recognize that we bring nothing to the table and are in great need of Jesus to meet the law's demands on our behalf.

Far from being a moral stepping stone, the law is the great crusher of pride and bruiser of ego; to use it for any other purpose is a corruption of God's intent. When we read the law, we are continually reminded of our great fortune in Jesus. We are pointed back to the gospel, time and time again, as we remember that Jesus has always been God's one and only plan for salvation:

> **"Therefore, there is now no condemnation for those who are in Christ Jesus, because through Christ Jesus the law of the Spirit of life set me free from the law of sin and death. For what the law was powerless to do in that it was weakened by the sinful nature, God did by sending his own Son in the likeness of sinful man to be a sin offering. And so he condemned sin in sinful man, in order that**

---

 12. For a sobering look at just how far short we fall of God's law, read Romans 3.

the righteous requirements of the law might be fully met in us, who do not live according to the sinful nature but according to the Spirit" (Romans 8:1-4, NIV).

Ironically, the law is really about the grace of God in Christ. For this reason, we should love and respect God's law, rather than neglect or abuse it. In order to do that, we must embrace the true purpose of the law—Jesus' perfection on behalf of our imperfections.

READ. THINK. DISCUSS.

Do you enjoy reading the Old Testament? Why or why not?

How should knowing the purpose of the law change the way we read and study it?

Why is it such a bad thing to use the law as a stepping stone to God?

Is God using the law in your life as a mirror or a window right now? How?

7.5 AMEN

Amen is a comforting word. But to most of us, it's not comforting because of its true meaning; it's comforting because it signals the end of a prayer, which is an ashamedly uncomfortable time. Saying "amen" has become little more than a Christian sign-off to God, an appropriate way to let the Almighty know that we deem our conversation with Him over. We say "amen" and move on with the rest of our lives.

Don't be fooled. That's not what *amen* really means at all.

WHOLEHEARTED AGREEMENT

Amen really means "I agree" or "may it be so." It's an affirmation of something that has been said or done. However, it's more than just a verbal assent to a factual statement. Amen has a certain weight behind it. When we say "amen," we are pledging our support for whatever has just been proposed. We are saying that we wholeheartedly agree with it, that it's our intense desire, even passion, to see said proposal come to pass. Perhaps we should be a little more careful with that word—or more emphatic.

Let's take our cue from the writers of Scripture.[13]

In Deuteronomy 27, the chapter of curses God laid out for disobedience, the people were instructed to shout "Amen!" after each individual curse as their whole-hearted affirmation and agreement. The people echoed the word in 1 Chronicles 16 when the ark of the covenant was brought into their presence and David sang his great psalm of thanksgiving. The word rings throughout the Psalms as the people's excited response to the praise of God. When we get to the New Testament, we see Paul closing many of his letters with the word.

In each of these cases, *amen* isn't just a Christian sign-off; it marks a sending-out moment. It's the word by which we signal our passionate agreement with what has been said. It's also our determination to go out from that moment of reading or worship into the world to live out what we learned and experienced.[14]

One of the most interesting places in Scripture we find the word *amen* is at the very end of the story. The apostle John, writer of the Book of Revelation, uses the word twice in the last two verses:

> **"He who testifies about these things says, 'Yes, I am coming quickly.'**
> **'Amen! Come, Lord Jesus!'**
> **The grace of the Lord Jesus be with all the saints. Amen"** (Revelation 22:20-21).

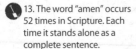 13. The word "amen" occurs 52 times in Scripture. Each time it stands alone as a complete sentence.

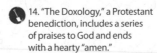 14. "The Doxology," a Protestant benediction, includes a series of praises to God and ends with a hearty "amen."

After his revelation of the end of days, John said "amen" to two specific things. The first was the second coming of the Lord Jesus. It might seem an obvious place to say amen. Of course we wholeheartedly anticipate Jesus' return. But Revelation isn't a sweet and warm book. In the previous chapters of Revelation, John described the terrible things that will happen before Jesus' return. His descriptions include dragons, beasts, destruction, and bowls of wrath. Saying "amen" to Jesus' return also means affirming the events leading up to the end times.

Despite all the things he prophesied about, John put a resounding amen at the end. May it be so! Bring on the locusts! Bring them on because the coming of all those things means that Jesus is drawing ever closer. That's what John was really saying amen to, for he knew that the coming of Jesus would make all those other things, and indeed all the pain of our present situations, fade into the distant background. May it be so.

But then John used the word one more time. At the *very* end. It's the last word in all of Scripture, a way of closing the book. And it is the only appropriate response to the Word of God.

AFFIRMING *ALL* OF SCRIPTURE
Sometimes we think of the Bible as segmented volumes of a book. We like the Gospels very much because we see them as the "grace and love" books. But all that stuff about war in the Old Testament? We don't care for it too much. So we center ourselves in those passages of Scripture that are the most spiritually palpable. But the Bible doesn't work like that.

It's not like God was mean and angry in the Old Testament and then somewhere in the 400 years between Malachi and Matthew, someone pulled Him aside and convinced Him to lighten up a bit. There is one God, perfectly unchanging for all time. The God of Abraham is the God of Paul; the God of Amos is the God of Luke.

If we really want to know this God, which we should since that's the true focus of Christianity, we must affirm all of Scripture, not just the easy parts. We must escape the cafeteria line approach to the Bible, where we pick and choose a few favorite verses here and there, and instead read it for what it is—the continual revelation of God.

That's why *amen* is the appropriate response at the end of Scripture. We say with John that we agree and support the entire thing. We affirm the truth contained in its pages, and we look to it as the basis for life and godliness. Sure, we need to grow in understanding certain parts of it, but we must accept it as it is. Every word of it.

When it comes to Scripture, we have two options: We say "amen" to its entirety, or we reject it entirely. No accepting it in parts; no dividing it in pieces. The commitment we have to

 Listen to "Wake Up, Oh Sleeper"
by Bear Rinehart, Jason Crabb,
and Jonathan Shelton from
the *Holy Vocabulary* playlist.

meditating on it, memorizing it, and dwelling inside the richness of its pages will affirm which choice we have made.

Such is the case with the holy vocabulary of faith. Although many of these words have become catch phrases within Christian circles and punch lines outside those circles, the great truth of knowing God and walking with Him rests inside a living understanding of these sacred words. And if we want to walk with God, we must say "amen" to them as well.

How about you? Ready to say the word? Ready to live the word?

May it be so. Amen.

END NOTES

SESSION 1

i. James Stuart Bell, *From the Library of C. S. Lewis* (WaterBrook Press, 2004), 11.

ii. Jen Hatmaker, *Interrupted: An Adventure in Relearning the Essentials of Faith* (Nashville: LifeWay Press, 2009), 71.

SESSION 2

iii. *http://thinkexist.com/quotation/i_have_never_been_lost-but_i_will_admit_to_being/175120.html*

iv. *http://womenshistory.about.com/od/quotes/a/madeleinelengle.htm*

SESSION 3

v. *http://www.beliefnet.com/Quotes/Christian/E/E-M-Bounds/All-Gods-Plans-Have-The-Mark-Of-The-Cross-On-Them.aspx?su=%2FFaiths%2FJudaism%2FJewish-Quote-Search.aspx%3Fq%3Dbible%26submitted%3Dyes%26p%3D25&tl=&sd=&ed=&q=bible*

vi. Philip Yancey, *What's So Amazing About Grace?* (Grand Rapids: Zondervan, 1997), 55.

SESSION 5

vii. Ed Stetzer, Richie Stanley, and Jason Hayes, *Lost and Found* (Nashville: B&H Publishing Group, 2009), 34.

viii. Lauren Winner, *Mudhouse Sabbath* (Brewster, Mass.: Paraclete Press, 2003), 68.

ix. Ed Stetzer, *Sent: Living the Missional Nature of the Church* (Nashville, LifeWay Press, 2008), 14.

SESSION 7

x. John Wesley, *Sermons on Several Occasions*, Vol. 1 (New York: Waugh & Mason, 1836), 6.

xi. *http://www.tentmaker.org/Quotes/biblequotes.htm*

xii. *http://www.tentmaker.org/Quotes/biblequotes.htm*

THE TOUGH SAYINGS OF JESUS II

MICHAEL KELLEY

LIMPING ALONG

"For God so loved the world . . ."

You know the rest. There are some statements that Jesus made that have gotten comfortable for us. They have become like a favorite T-shirt, well-worn and broken in. We put them on because they feel good. They are familiar. We like the way they look—and we should.

"God so loved the world" is no less true today than it was in some back room of a Palestinian house 2,000 years ago when Jesus first said it. God still loves the world. He did give His one and only Son to pave the way for people to come back to Him. That's completely legitimate.

That is, however, not the only thing Jesus said. He said lots of stuff, and much of it isn't quite as easy to wear as that famous verse from John. He called a woman a dog. He told a rich, young ruler that he could work his way to heaven. He said He was glad a good friend of His was dead. It's those words of Jesus that don't fit quite as comfortably as the 3:16 shirt. But when we neglect the fullness of what Jesus said—when we only think about those things that are comfortable for us to consider—then we are living up to the famous definition

When we only think about those things that are comfortable for us to consider, we are living up to the famous definition that Karl Marx gave to religion in general. In his words, religion is "the opium of the people." We use our religion—in this case, Christianity—to make ourselves feel better.

that Karl Marx gave to religion in general. In his words, religion is "the opium of the people." We use our religion—in this case, Christianity—to make ourselves feel better.

But is that really wrong? I mean, there's enough stuff in the world to make us feel bad. Between disease, poverty, political injustice, and all the other everyday problems of life, surely it's not wrong to look to Jesus to feel better.

That's not wrong really. Jesus did say that He came so that His followers would not only have life, but have an incredibly full life—an abundant one. So in a sense, Jesus does make us feel better, but His definition of that is much different than ours. Too often we are guilty of thinking that life with Jesus is somehow supposed to be easier—more comfortable—than life without Him.

I wonder what those twelve disciples who first walked with Him would say about that. Those guys who heard Him first talk about the abundant life that comes along with Him are the same ones who spent their lives undergoing persecution and hardship. Many lived without homes. Eleven were killed for their faith. So how is that life abundant?

You could answer that question in a lot of ways. It's abundant because of the peace of knowing that God is in control. It's abundant because you know your life is about something bigger than yourself. It's abundant because lasting joy can really only be found in God through Christ. It's abundant because with Jesus, there is the promise of another life—an eternal one—that will make this one seem like a hazy dream. And then there's this: Life with Jesus is abundant because it is life lived deeply.

I think we all want that last one. We want to walk deeply with Jesus. That walk is deeply satisfying. It's deeply abundant. It's deeply mysterious in a very good way. The hard part about walking deeply with the Son of God (so I've heard from those who do) is that it's also deeply uncomfortable.

The road to a deep, authentic walk with Christ looks different for everyone, but I think most of those roads have similar characteristics. Many of them involve a season of extreme difficulty usually because of life circumstances. More of them involve a commitment to practicing the classic spiritual disciplines that position us to receive truth from the hand of God. And all of them require an ever-increasing commitment to faith and obedience. But all of these characteristics also have this in common—they are a struggle.

That's what I hope this volume of **Tough Sayings** is for you and me both. I hope it's a chance for us to be discontent with what is comfortable and to struggle with a Jesus who refuses to be domesticated by modern church standards. I hope it creates dialogue about what it really means to walk along life's journey with Christ in a deeper fashion.

It reminds me a little of the fascinatingly bizarre Old Testament story of Jacob, the shifty, deceptive son of Isaac. He spent a night wrestling with an angel of the Lord (or perhaps God, depending on who you talk to). And after that night he was different. He emerged with a new name and a new blessing because he "struggled with God and with men and . . . prevailed" (Genesis 32:28). But he also came out with something else: a limp. His walk was changed forever because of those moments he spent grappling with the Lord.

Maybe the same thing can happen to us. Wrestling isn't easy; it's certainly not comfortable. And we will be marked because of having done it. We will walk differently than we did before. But that struggle is part of a walk with Jesus who is not defined by comfort and ease; it's defined by the unsafe, unconventional, controversial Son of God.

Read on. Question. Process. Wrestle. And hopefully limp.

We want to walk deeply with Jesus. That walk is deeply satisfying. It's deeply abundant. It's deeply mysterious in a very good way. The hard part about walking deeply with the Son of God is that it's also deeply uncomfortable . . .

Read on. Question. Process. Wrestle. And hopefully limp.

WHAT IS THREADS?

WE ARE A COMMUNITY OF YOUNG ADULTS—

people who are piecing the Christian life together, one experience at a time. Threads is driven by four key markers that are essential to young adults everywhere, and though it's always dangerous to categorize people, we think these are helpful in reminding us why we do what we do.

First of all, we are committed to being responsible. That is, doing the right thing. Though we're trying to grow in our understanding of what that is, we're glad we already know what to do when it comes to recycling, loving our neighbor, tithing, or giving of our time.

Community is also important to us. We believe we all need people. People we call when the tire's flat and people we call when we get the promotion. And it's those people—the day-in-day-out people—that we want to walk through life with.

Then there's connection. A connection with our church, a connection with somebody who's willing to walk along side us and give us a little advice here and there. We'd like a connection that gives us the opportunity to pour our lives out for somebody else—and that whole walk along side us thing, we're willing to do that for someone else, too.

And finally there's depth. Kiddie pools are for kids. We're looking to dive in, head first, to all the hard-to-talk-about topics, the tough questions, and heavy Scriptures. We're thinking this is a good thing, because we're in process. We're becoming. And who we're becoming isn't shallow.

We're glad you're here. Be sure and check us out online at:

THREADSMEDIA.COM

STOP BY TO JOIN OUR ONLINE COMMUNITY — AND COME BY TO VISIT OFTEN!

174